Gifts from the Kitchen

Gifts from the Kitchen

KASEY WILSON

Douglas & McIntyre
Vancouver/Toronto

Douglas & McIntyre Ltd., 1615 Venables Street, Vancouver, British Columbia   V5L 2H1

Canadian Cataloguing in Publication Data

Wilson, Kasey
Gifts from the kitchen

Includes index.
ISBN 0-88894-571-X
1. Cookery, Canadian. 2. Cookery. 3. Gifts.
I. Title.
TX715.W457 1987   641.5971   C87-091337-9

Design and art direction by Barbara Hodgson
Photography by Derik Murray
Colour separations by Cleland-Kent Western Ltd.
Typeset by The Typeworks
Printed and bound in Canada by Hemlock Printers Ltd.

For my twin sister,
Karen May
my mother, Peggy Byron
my grandmother, Charlotte Byron
and especially my daughter,
Karen Meagan Wilson

CONTENTS

ACKNOWLEDGEMENTS

The author and the publisher gratefully acknowledge the generous assistance and support of Meagher's Distillery Ltd. and the Four Seasons Hotel, Vancouver.

A special thank you to Sue Kelly for her encouragement through every phase of this book; Stevie Mitchell for her creative appetite; Jim Poirier for his wonderfully innovative ideas; Ruy Paes Braga for his continuing support; Judith Filtness for her patience and preparation of the manuscript, and Lori Ramsden for her diligent work in the metrication of these recipes.

Many friends contributed to this book in many different ways, some with recipes and others with support. My thanks to all of them and in particular: Mae Adams, T. K. Bakar, Jacquie Cherot, Mae Livingstone, Alison MacLennan, Claudia Roden, Marlene Sorosky, Diana and Paul Von Welanetz and last but not least, Julie Watson.

GIVING GIFTS

Cooking and giving gifts are pleasures, especially when you give to friends the delicious foods that you make in your own kitchen. In this book you'll find recipes designed to be made and given as gifts. You'll also find suggestions and other recipes to enclose with your homemade preserves and sauces, so that recipients will know how to serve them. And you'll find helpful ideas on putting together unique gift packages that include homemade and store-bought specialty foods, complementary nonfood items and interesting containers.

The recipes in this book are drawn from many cuisines and are exciting enough for the adventurous yet straightforward enough for the novice or recreational cook. Whatever your time and inclination, you can prepare a gift of food. You can spend just a few minutes combining a few ingredients to make a fancy fruit vinegar (and attach a recipe for using it in a high-fashion dressing), or you can be grandiose and prepare a complete dinner for a truly special celebration.

Giving gifts of food combines the warmth of tradition with the spirit of inventiveness. You can get your family to don aprons so that everyone can cook with ease and enthusiasm to produce gifts. Or you can share the kitchen with a friend or two, splitting the costs, effort and results. What's more, if you prepare fruits and vegetables when they are in season—by refrigerating, freezing, canning and other make-ahead techniques—you can stage manage an impressive amount of food to give as gifts all year round. You can also look ahead by assembling and preparing baked goods, sauces and mixes when you find bargains in the marketplace. And don't forget the benefits of delivering your gift of food yourself—you'll often be invited to stay and share it along with a glass of good cheer.

To package and present your gifts, keep your eyes open for items that might serve as attractive containers and accompaniments. Auctions, flea markets and garage sales are perfect places for collecting escargot dishes, covered soup bowls, stoneware crocks and unusual decanters. Import, discount and hardware stores often have great buys on baskets, boxes, casseroles, mugs, glassware, napkins and platters. Florist and gardening shops have terra cotta pots and planters, as well as watering cans. Toy stores sell small supermarket carts and wheelbarrows, lunch pails and tiny refrigerators. Go to cookware shops and lay in a store of inexpensive canisters in different sizes and small utensils such as zesters, whisks, pasta forks or pizza cutters—you'll find that the gadget section has a fascinating array. Once you get started, you'll come up with your own ideas.

Remember to label foods with necessary information on storage and serving suggestions, as well as cooking, freezing or reheating instructions. You may also want to enclose the recipe itself so the recipient can produce another batch.

Make the labels and recipes attractive by typing, printing, or gluing photocopies of recipes and serving suggestions onto coloured file or recipe cards, decals, or decorative notepaper. Cookbook, cookware and stationery shops are good sources for cards and labels.

Over time, collect an assortment of wrapping paper, ribbons and bows so that you're always prepared.

Some general ideas for putting together interesting, personalized packages are outlined below, and more specific ideas tied to particular recipes appear in appropriate spots throughout the book. But these are just suggestions to start you thinking, to inspire you to make food gifts and present them with flair.

Here are some ideas for special occasions:

To salute a promotion, fill a portable cardboard file box with two champagne glasses containing Boysenberry Truffles, a bottle of champagne, and perhaps caviar, a cigar, an abacus or a pocket calculator. You could also add the *Financial Times, Barrons, Fortune* magazine or a business book on the best-seller list.

To celebrate the birth of a baby, fill a doll's cradle or toy truck with a loaf of Irish Wheaten Bread, a jar of Maple Butter and Fruit in Liqueur. Add a cigar and one or more of the following: a week's supply of bibs, the latest book on child-rearing, a children's book or small toy. Tie it all together with a cheerful ribbon.

To honour an engagement or marriage, fill an old-fashioned twig basket with Petite Licorelle (a sparkling liqueur), a set of Designer Snacks and a jar of Amaretto Praline Sauce. Add a book of love poems, a copy of *Architectural Digest,* a paperback on relationships or *Picnics for Lovers* by Gabrielle Kirschbaum.

To celebrate moving into a new home, put together a warm welcome for the new occupants to enjoy: Market Chowder, Cornbread Buttermilk Muffins, Bell Pepper Butter, Hot Basil Vinegar, and the recipe and fixings for Tomato Mozzarella Salad—all packed in a basket lined with a set of calico napkins. Add a glass cylinder filled with Iced Double-Chocolate Cookies.

You'll always be a welcome guest, whatever the season, when you arrive with homemade delicacies to lighten the load of your host or hostess:

For boaters, who must deal with the limitations of a galley, pack Narsai's Duck Liver Pâté or Winnipeg Goldeye Pâté or

Stilton Pâté in an inexpensive plastic container. Put in a bag of bagel chips with your pâté. Add a container of chilled Pumpkin Soup covered with an airtight lid. Fill a metal tin with cookies or wrap a small loaf of Peach Fruitcake in foil.

For a summer cottage weekend, take beer and a cooler packed with Stilton Pâté, Parmesan Herbed Bread, cold Cajun Drumsticks, Jalapeño Potato Salad and Black Beast for dessert.

For a day of hiking or cross-country skiing, deliver a backpack filled with Italian picnic food: two jars of Carrot Artichoke Antipasto, Italian rolls and cold cuts, Gorgonzola or provolone cheese and a bottle of Chianti. Add a thermos of hot espresso and some Italian cookies or chocolate. You may want to tuck in a gift of a Swiss army knife or a compass.

For an elegant Parisian picnic, fill a French wire egg basket with Narsai's Duck Liver Pâté, a fresh baguette, Brie and Roquefort cheeses, a bottle of French wine and some fresh fruit. Tie a big red, white and blue bow on the side of the basket and attach a small, inexpensive French cooking tool to the bow. For a special friend, enclose one of the following: a good French cookbook such as *Mastering the Art of French Cooking* or Jacques Pepin's cooking video, a copy of *Paris Match* or *Passion* magazine. Or pick up a French film at a video rental shop on the way to your friend's place and settle in for an evening of relaxation.

For a Labour Day weekend picnic, make chilled Pumpkin Soup. Transport the soup in and serve it from a pumpkin shell, which will also act as an insulator to keep it cool.

For a fall occasion use an old-fashioned tea tray to present a crock of Stilton Pâté, English biscuits, a bottle of vintage port and an Agatha Christie murder mystery or a travel book on Britain.

Special holidays call for special treats:

A white Christmas: make an array of white gifts that are savoury and sweet. For savouries, make Baked Garlic Dip,

Stilton Pâté and Dill Toast Hearts. For sweets, put a jar of Amaretto Praline Sauce and French vanilla ice cream in a white styrofoam cooler. Tie with a festive bow.

A rich Christmas: make Peach Fruitcake or Iced Rum Cake with Eggnog Sauce. Or combine small versions of both in a sampler with some other cakes and cookies.

New Year's Day: give advance notice and deliver a brunch to food-loving friends. Pack a jar of Blueberry Chutney, then make up your favourite pancake or waffle recipe, leaving out the liquid ingredients. Put in instructions to combine 2 cups of the dry mixture with the liquid ingredients, then to fold in ½ cup of the chutney. To top off the pancakes or waffles, pack some fresh or thawed frozen berries and a jar of Crème Fraîche. And don't forget to put in some freshly baked croissants or muffins from your local bakery, as well as a thermos of hot espresso or a special blend of tea.

Valentine's Day: a time to celebrate fond friends, new loves and old passions. For all or any of the above, create a romantic interlude with a long-stemmed red rose in an individual water tube and a bottle of Petite Licorelle in a basket. Wrap a red bow around the neck of the bottle. Add two champagne flutes filled with Boysenberry Truffles, a cassette tape of some suitable music and unplug the phone.

Gifts from the Garden

When your summer garden
or local farmers' market
is overflowing
with an abundance of fruits,
vegetables and herbs,
be prepared with these recipes
to produce gifts of preserves
for all occasions.

CHUTNEYS

Preserves are easier to make than you think. Many of the chutneys and other preserves in this book may simply be refrigerated rather than be put through the traditional canning process. If you do make refrigerated preserves, there is no need to use canning jars—any sterilized glass jars will do. But make sure, perhaps on the label, that gift recipients understand these are not canned preserves, so must be kept refrigerated. If you plan to use the traditional way, please read "About Canning" (p. 120) before you start.

Pear Chutney

10 cups	peeled, cored, sliced pears (about 5 lbs./2.3 kg)	2.5 L
½ cup	green pepper, chopped	125 mL
1½ cups	raisins	375 mL
4 cups	sugar	1 L
1 cup	crystallized ginger, chopped	250 mL
3 cups	cider vinegar	750 mL
½ tsp.	salt	2 mL
½ tsp.	whole cloves	2 mL
½ tsp.	whole allspice	2 mL
3 3-inch sticks	cinnamon	3 7.5-cm sticks

1. In a heavy saucepan, combine pears, pepper, raisins, sugar, ginger, vinegar and salt.
2. Tie cloves, allspice and cinnamon sticks in double thickness of cheesecloth and place in saucepan.
3. Heat pear mixture to boiling, stirring frequently.

Reduce heat and simmer 1½–2 hours or until chutney is dark and syrupy. Stir frequently to prevent scorching.

4. Remove spice bag and ladle chutney into sterilized jars, cool and refrigerate. Or ladle chutney into 4 one-cup (250-mL) sterilized canning jars, leaving ¼-inch (6-mm) headspace, and process for 10 minutes (see "About Canning," p. 120).

5. Label jars, attach the Serving Suggestions and the recipe for Chutney Mayonnaise.

Makes 1 quart (1 L).

Variations: To make Peach Chutney, use 10 cups (2.5 L) of peeled, pitted, chopped peaches.

To make Plum Chutney, use 15 cups (3.75 L) of unpeeled, pitted, chopped blue plums.

SERVING SUGGESTIONS
Refrigerate, keeps about a year. Serve with curry dishes, on muffins, in pancake and waffle batter or heated and spooned over ice cream. Try making Chutney Mayonnaise according to the attached recipe

Chutney Mayonnaise

1 cup	commercial mayonnaise	250 mL
1 cup	sour cream	250 mL
3 Tbsp.	Pear, Peach or Plum Chutney	50 mL
1 Tbsp.	curry paste OR	15 mL
4 tsp.	curry powder	20 mL

Combine all ingredients and refrigerate overnight for flavours to ripen. Store in refrigerator, keeps 2 weeks.

Makes 1 pint (500 mL).

A delicious combination of chutney and curry to dress a salad of shrimp and fresh pineapple or honeydew melon or cantaloupe; or sliced chicken breast with mango.

Blueberry Chutney

1½ cups	maple-flavoured syrup	375 mL
1½ cups	blueberries	375 mL
3	medium apples, peeled and chopped	3
¾ cup	raisins	175 mL
½ cup	pecans	125 mL
¼ cup	lemon juice	50 mL
1 tsp.	salt	5 mL
1 Tbsp.	chopped onion	15 mL
¼ tsp.	ground cloves	1 mL

1. In a medium saucepan, combine all ingredients and bring to a boil, stirring frequently. Reduce heat and simmer uncovered 40 minutes or until mixture thickens. Stir frequently to avoid scorching.

2. Ladle into sterilized jars, cool and refrigerate. Or ladle into 4 one-cup (250-mL) sterilized canning jars, leaving ¼-inch (6-mm) headspace, and process for 10 minutes (see "About Canning," p. 120).

3. Label jars, attach the Serving Suggestions and the recipe for Blueberry Chutney Sorbet.

Makes 1 quart (1 L).

SERVING SUGGESTIONS

Refrigerate, keeps about a year. Serve with curry dishes, on muffins, in pancake and waffle batter or heated and spooned over ice cream; or layer chutney in a trifle; or create an unusual sorbet with the attached recipe.

Blueberry Chutney Sorbet

½ cup	sugar	125 mL
1 ½ cups	water	375 mL
2 cups	Blueberry Chutney, puréed	500 mL
1	egg white (for freezer method only)	1
1 Tbsp.	sugar (for freezer method only)	15 mL
½ cup	Grand Marnier OR orange liqueur	125 mL

Combine sugar and water in a small saucepan and boil for 5 minutes. Cool completely.

FREEZER METHOD
Add sugar syrup to Blueberry Chutney and mix thoroughly. Beat egg white, gradually adding sugar, until stiff peaks form. Fold egg mixture into fruit and pour into a metal pan to a depth of 1 inch (2.5 cm). Freeze for about 3 hours.

   Remove mixture from freezer. When it becomes mushy, transfer to a mixing bowl. Add Grand Marnier and beat with an electric mixer until fluffy. Return sorbet to pan and freeze 1 hour or until firm. If sorbet becomes too hard, remove it from the freezer about 15 minutes before serving.

ELECTRIC ICE CREAM MAKER METHOD
Combine Blueberry Chutney, sugar syrup and Grand Marnier and place in ice cream maker. Freeze according to manufacturer's directions.
   Makes 1 quart (1 L).

Sorbet is perfect between courses to cleanse the palate. Prepare just a few hours before serving or it will become too icy to scoop.

Lemon Apricot Chutney

2 cups	halved lemon slices	500 mL
1 cup	dried apricots, coarsely chopped	250 mL
1 cup	golden raisins	250 mL
1 cup	chopped onions	250 mL
1½ cups	sugar	375 mL
1½ cups	cider vinegar	375 mL
3 Tbsp.	chopped candied ginger	50 mL
½ tsp.	ground allspice	2 mL
1 tsp.	salt	5 mL

1. In a medium-large saucepan, combine all ingredients and bring to a boil. Reduce heat and simmer covered for 1 hour. Uncover and simmer 30 minutes longer or until thickened.

2. Ladle chutney into sterilized jars, cool and refrigerate. Or ladle chutney into 4 one-cup (250-mL) sterilized canning jars, leaving ¼-inch (6-mm) headspace, and process for 10 minutes (see "About Canning," p. 120).

3. Label jars, attach the Serving Suggestions and the recipe for Lemon Apricot Chutney Sorbet.

Makes 1 quart (1 L).

SERVING SUGGESTIONS

Refrigerate, keeps about a year. Wonderful as a glaze for ham or blended with yogurt to dress a fruit salad. Use it as a relish to perk up mild foods, or create an unusual sorbet with the attached recipe.

Lemon Apricot Chutney Sorbet 🍲

½ cup	sugar	125 mL
1½ cups	water	375 mL
2 cups	Lemon Apricot Chutney, puréed	500 mL
1	egg white (for freezer method only)	1
1 Tbsp.	sugar (for freezer method only)	15 mL
½ cup	Armagnac	125 mL

Combine sugar and water in a small saucepan and boil for 5 minutes. Cool completely.

FREEZER METHOD
Add sugar syrup to Lemon Apricot Chutney and mix thoroughly. Beat egg white, gradually adding sugar, until stiff peaks form. Fold egg mixture into fruit and pour into a metal pan to a depth of 1 inch (2.5 cm). Freeze for about 3 hours.

Remove mixture from freezer. When it becomes mushy, transfer to a mixing bowl. Add Armagnac and beat with an electric mixer until fluffy. Return sorbet to pan and freeze 1 hour or until firm. If sorbet becomes too hard, remove it from the freezer about 15 minutes before serving.

ELECTRIC ICE CREAM MAKER METHOD
Combine Lemon Apricot Chutney, sugar syrup and Armagnac and add to ice cream maker. Freeze according to manufacturer's directions.

Makes 1 quart (1 L).

Sorbet is perfect between courses to cleanse the palate. Prepare just a few hours before serving or it will become too icy to scoop.

DRESSINGS AND VINEGARS

Tall glass carafes, corked and tied with ribbon, make elegant containers for homemade dressings and vinegars. Or present them in recycled half-size liqueur and wine bottles, recycled Perrier bottles or 1-quart (1-L) wine carafes. Purchase a supply of corks from a wine-making shop and insert the corks into the bottles.

For a professional-looking presentation of vinegars, use plastic capsules called Enotherms, available in wine-making shops; when steamed over a kettle, they shrink over the necks of corked bottles. They come in various colours.

Dressing Rack. Place Maple Mustard Dressing and Karen's Creamy Caesar Dressing in half-size wine or champagne bottles and place them in a small wooden wine rack. Add a bottle of Fresh Fruit Vinegar, olive oil and a half-bottle of wine. Pass along your favourite salad recipes with the dressings, or a salad cookbook such as *Salad* by Amy Nathan.

Potted preserves: Present one or more homemade chutneys, vinegars, jams, jellies and relishes in a terra cotta flowerpot. Fill it about halfway with packing straw or tissue paper, then add the labelled jars and bottles.

Add a small bottle of Italian extra-virgin olive oil, or a basil or rosemary plant. You may also want to include a copy of your favourite food magazine, such as *The Pleasure of Cooking.*

Place the pot in the centre of a large square of clear cellophane, bring up the corners of the cellophane and use an elastic band to hold together. Tie a large ribbon around the elastic band, make a bow and attach a small gardening tool.

Glorious Foods' Sherried Dressing

4 cups	commercial mayonnaise	1 L
½ cup	sherry	125 mL
2 Tbsp.	finely chopped garlic	25 mL
1 tsp.	salt	5 mL
1 tsp.	coarsely ground pepper	5 mL
½ cup	blue cheese	125 mL

1. Combine all ingredients in a food processor with a metal blade and process until smooth.

2. Transfer to 2 one-pint (500-mL) carafes, cork, label and refrigerate. Attach Serving Suggestions before presenting.

Makes 5 cups (1.25 L).

SERVING SUGGESTIONS
Store in refrigerator for a maximum of 1 month. Serve on a wedge of crisp iceberg or romaine lettuce and sprinkle with chopped walnuts or pecans.

One of Vancouver's most popular caterers developed this recipe.

A special treat from my twin sister's cooking school.

Karen's Creamy Caesar Dressing

½	large lemon	½
2	egg yolks	2
3 drops	Tabasco sauce	3 drops
2 cloves	garlic, minced	2 cloves
2 Tbsp.	Dijon mustard	25 mL
3–5 Tbsp.	sour cream	50–75 mL
2-oz. can	flat fillets of anchovies	50-g can
	salt and freshly ground pepper	
1 cup	olive oil	250 mL

1. Squeeze juice from lemon half.
2. Place the lemon juice, egg yolks, Tabasco sauce, garlic, mustard, sour cream, anchovies, salt and pepper in a food processor or blender with a metal blade and process until smooth. With the machine running, slowly add the oil through the feeder tube in a thin, steady stream. It will thicken like whipping cream. (If you are using a blender, you may have to prepare this recipe in two batches.)
3. Pour into a 1-pint (500-mL) carafe, cork, label and refrigerate. Attach Serving Suggestions before presenting.

Makes 1 pint (500 mL).

SERVING SUGGESTIONS
Serve with romaine lettuce, croutons and freshly grated Parmesan cheese for the best Caesar salad ever. Store in refrigerator for up to 2 weeks.

Potted Condiments: In the pot on the left are Blueberry Chutney and Hot Basil Vinegar, with fresh sweet peppers and garlic; to the left are a gardening tool and a basil plant; beside the pot are Quince Jelly, olive oil, Fresh Fruit Vinegar, Hot Pepper Jelly, Torshi, and Peach and Pepper Relish. All can be packaged with fresh fruits and vegetables from your garden.

Maple Mustard Dressing

1 cup	mayonnaise	250 mL
1 cup	Dijon mustard	250 mL
¾ cup	vinegar	175 mL
3 Tbsp.	sugar	50 mL
2 cloves	garlic, minced	2 cloves
1 tsp.	white pepper	5 mL
½ tsp.	ground cloves	2 mL
½ tsp.	Tabasco sauce	2 mL
1 cup	maple syrup	250 mL
1¾ cup	olive oil	425 mL
1 Tbsp.	poppy seeds	15 mL
¼ cup	chopped cilantro	50 mL

Cilantro is also known as Chinese parsley or coriander.

1. In a food processor with a metal blade, combine mayonnaise, mustard, vinegar, sugar, garlic, pepper, cloves, Tabasco sauce and maple syrup. Process for 5 seconds, stopping to scrape the sides of the bowl.

2. With the machine running, slowly add the oil through the feeder tube in a thin, steady stream. Add poppy seeds and cilantro and process a further 3 seconds.

3. Pour into 3 one-pint (500-mL) carafes, cork, label and refrigerate. Attach Serving Suggestions before presenting.

Makes 1½ quarts (1.5 L).

SERVING SUGGESTIONS
Use as a dressing for spinach salads, fruit salads or vegetable slaws. Store in refrigerator. Keeps one week.

Parisian Picnic Fare: In the egg basket are Pommery Moutarde Royale, Roquefort and Brie cheeses, Dubonnet and a baguette, with a French dictionary, a travel diary, tea towels and wooden spoons; in the crock is Narsai's Duck Liver Pâté.

Hot Basil Vinegar

1 qt.	white OR red wine vinegar	1 L
5	long sprigs fresh basil	5
10	black peppercorns	10

1. Pour vinegar into 2 one-pint (500-mL) bottles or 1 one-quart (1-L) bottle. Add basil and peppercorns, being careful not to break basil sprigs.

2. Cork and label bottles and let stand in dark cool place about 2 weeks. Attach recipe for Tomato Mozzarella Salad.

Makes 1 quart (1 L).

Tomato Mozzarella Salad

½ cup	Hot Basil Vinegar	125 mL
⅔ cup	olive oil	150 mL
1 tsp.	salt	5 mL
2	medium tomatoes, sliced	2
¼ lb.	fresh mozzarella cheese, cut into 4 slices	125 g
1 head	butter lettuce	1 head
3 Tbsp.	red onion, chopped	50 mL

Whisk together vinegar, oil and salt. Arrange tomatoes and cheese on butter lettuce and sprinkle with red onion. Drizzle dressing over salad.

Serves 4.

Honey Rosemary Vinegar

1½ cups	white wine vinegar	375 mL
1 Tbsp.	honey	15 mL
½ cup	seedless grapes	125 mL
1	large sprig rosemary	1

1. Combine vinegar and honey in small saucepan. Heat until honey is dissolved. Place grapes and rosemary in a 1-pint (500-mL) bottle and pour in warmed vinegar.

2. Cork and label bottle and let stand several days. Attach recipe for Mixed Greens with Raspberries and Toasted Pine Nuts.

Makes 1 pint (500 mL).

Mixed Greens with Raspberries and Toasted Pine Nuts

⅜ cup	Honey Rosemary Vinegar	100 mL
½ cup	olive oil	125 mL
1 head	butter lettuce	1 head
1 head	endive	1 head
1 bunch	watercress	1 bunch
1 cup	raspberries	250 mL
2 Tbsp.	toasted pine nuts	30 mL

Whisk vinegar into oil. Assemble a salad of butter lettuce, endive, watercress, raspberries and pine nuts. Drizzle dressing on salad.

Serves 4—6.

Fresh Fruit Vinegar

3 qts.	raspberries, peaches, plums OR cherries	3 L
2 cups	white wine vinegar	500 mL
	sugar	

1. Rinse fruit. Drain and crush to release the juices. Place fruit in a glass bowl and cover with wine vinegar for 24 hours.
2. Strain the vinegar through cheesecloth or fine mesh. Measure liquid and mix with an equal amount of sugar. Place in stainless steel or enamel saucepan and bring to boil. Reduce heat and simmer 10 minutes. Let stand overnight, covered.
3. Decant vinegar into two 1½-cup (375-mL) bottles, cork and label. Store in a dark place for at least 2 weeks. Attach the recipe for Chicken and Fruit Salad.

Makes 3 cups (750 mL).

Chicken and Fruit Salad

6	chicken breasts, halved, deboned and skinned	6
½ cup	Fresh Fruit Vinegar	125 mL
⅔ cup	olive oil	150 mL
1 tsp.	sugar	5 mL
1 tsp.	powdered ginger	5 mL
1 head	leafy red lettuce	1 head
2 cups	strawberries OR raspberries, blueberries, grapes, kiwifruit OR a combination of fruits	500 mL

1. Poach chicken breasts by placing them in a single layer in a shallow, wide pan such as a large skillet. Add just enough liquid (salted water, chicken broth, white wine or a combination of these) to cover. Bring to a boil and reduce heat immediately. Cover and simmer 12 minutes or until chicken breasts are moist and just beyond the pink stage. Remove from liquid and cool to room temperature. Slice.

2. Prepare fruit vinaigrette by whisking together vinegar, oil, sugar and ginger.

3. Arrange sliced chicken breasts on lettuce-lined plates and surround with fruit.

4. Dress with fruit vinaigrette.

Serves 6.

JELLIES AND JAMS

In order to determine whether a jelly has reached the gelling point, use one of the following methods: dip a cool metal spoon in boiling jelly, then carry it out of the steam and pour from the spoon—the liquid should pour in a sheet; or pour a small amount of boiling jelly on a cold plate and place in freezer—when it has cooled, check to see if it has gelled.

Quince Jelly

3½ lbs.	quinces	1.5 kg
½	lemon	½
5 cups	sugar	1.25 L

1. Wash, quarter and remove stems and bruises from quinces.

2. Place fruit in stainless steel saucepan and add just enough water to cover. Bring to boil and cook over medium heat for 20 minutes or until fruit is soft.

3. Mash the fruit and pour into a damp jelly bag (or onto several layers of cheesecloth in a colander) set over a bowl so that the juice runs freely. Allow fruit to drain for at least 1 hour, or overnight. Reserve juice.

4. Squeeze juice from lemon half and strain juice.

5. Measure 4 cups (1 L) of quince juice into a stainless steel saucepan. Bring to a boil and cook for 5 minutes. Add lemon juice and sugar and stir only until dissolved. Boil rapidly for 10 minutes or until it reaches the gelling point.

6. With a metal spoon dipped in very hot water, skim off the foam. For long-term storage (about a year), ladle jelly into 4 one-cup (250-mL) sterilized canning jars, filling jars ⅛ inch (3 mm) from the top. Seal and invert 1 minute. For short-term storage (two months), use a ⅛-inch (3-mm) melted paraffin cover.

7. Label jars and attach the Serving Suggestion.

Makes 1 quart (1 L).

SERVING SUGGESTION
Best with toasted English muffins. Refrigerate after opening.

This round to pear-shaped autumn fruit is fully ripe when it is golden yellow. It is very sour in its raw state, but makes wonderful jellies and preserves when cooked.

Crabapple and Bell Pepper Jelly

3½ lbs.	crabapples	1.5 kg
⅓ cup	vinegar	75 mL
2 Tbsp.	mixed pickling spice (in cheesecloth bag)	25 mL
3	large sweet green peppers, seeded and cut into eighths	3
3	large sweet red peppers, seeded and cut into eighths	3
3–4 cups	white sugar	750 mL–1 L

1. To make juice from crabapples, wash, quarter and remove stems and bruises from fruit. Place fruit in stainless steel saucepan and add water to cover. Bring to a boil and cook over medium heat for 20 minutes or until fruit is soft. Mash the fruit and pour into a damp jelly bag (or several layers of cheesecloth in a colander) set over a bowl so that the juice runs freely. Allow fruit to drain for a minimum of 1 hour, or leave jelly bag overnight. Reserve juice.

2. Simmer 4 cups (1 L) of the drained juice, vinegar and spice bag in stainless steel saucepan for 10 minutes. Chop peppers in food processor using metal blade and add to sugar. Remove spice bag from juice mixture and add peppers and sugar and stir until sugar dissolves. Boil rapidly for 10 minutes or until it reaches the gelling point.

3. Skim off the foam using a spoon dipped in very hot water. For long-term storage (about a year), ladle jelly into 4 one-cup (250-mL) sterilized canning jars, leaving ⅛ inch (3 mm) headspace. Seal and invert 1 minute. For short-term storage (two months), use a ⅛-inch (3-mm) melted paraffin cover.

4. Label jars and attach the Serving Suggestions.
Makes 1 quart (1 L).

Rhubarb Ginger Jam

2 lbs.	rhubarb, washed, trimmed and cut into 1-inch (2.5-cm) pieces	1 kg
3¼ cups	sugar	800 mL
½ cup	crystallized ginger, chopped	125 mL
4 dashes	Tabasco sauce	4 dashes
¼ cup	fresh lemon juice	50 mL

Choose pinkish-red rhubarb that is firm and crisp.

1. Combine rhubarb, sugar, ginger, Tabasco sauce and lemon juice in a large saucepan and mix well. Place over medium heat and bring to a boil. Stirring frequently, simmer 30 minutes or until mixture is thick. Remove foam with metal spoon that has been dipped in very hot water.

2. Ladle into 4 one-cup (250-mL) sterilized canning jars and cover at once with ⅛ inch (3 mm) hot paraffin.

3. Label jars and attach the Serving Suggestion.
Makes 1 quart (1 L).

SERVING SUGGESTION
Serve with warmed croissants. Refrigerate after opening. Keeps 2 months after date of making.

Hot Pepper Jelly

This recipe, from my Granville Island Cookbook, *uses green peppers and green food colouring for green jelly, red peppers and red food colouring for red jelly.*

1 cup	sweet green OR red peppers, seeded and chopped	250 mL
¼ cup	fresh OR canned jalapeño peppers	50 mL
1¼ cups	apple cider vinegar	300 mL
6 cups	sugar	1.5 L
6-oz. bottle	Certo liquid fruit pectin	170-mL bottle
8 or 9 drops	red OR green food colouring	8 or 9 drops

1. First, read "About Chili Peppers" on p. 119. In a blender or food processor with a metal blade, combine sweet peppers, jalapeño peppers and about half of the vinegar. Process until smooth.

2. Pour the mixture into a large stainless steel saucepan. Rinse the blender with the remaining vinegar and add it to the peppers. Stir in the sugar. Bring mixture to a full, rolling boil and boil hard for 1 minute. Remove from heat and let stand 5 minutes. Skim off the foam.

3. Add Certo and food colouring. Stir until blended. Pour into 6 one-cup (250-mL) sterilized jars, label and refrigerate.

Makes 6 cups (1.5 L).

SERVING SUGGESTIONS

Serve as an accompaniment to chicken, pork or lamb, or on cream cheese and crackers. Store in refrigerator. Keeps about a year.

RELISHES

You might want to add some shish-kebab skewers or incense with the Torshi (Middle Eastern pickled turnips), or pack a selection of the relishes in a cast-iron hibachi. Wrap with cellophane and a bright ribbon.

Relish Basket. Present a friend with a selection of relishes. Place them in a colourful Mexican basket lined with bright tissue paper. Tie the Serving Suggestions around the necks of jars or bottles with jute string.

Torshi

Throughout the Middle East pickled vegetables called torshi are displayed in huge jars and decorate the windows and counters of most restaurants. They are made attractively pink or red by the addition of sliced raw beets or beet juice.

2 lbs.	small white turnips, peeled	1 kg
2–4 cloves	garlic	2–4 cloves
1	raw beet, peeled and sliced	1
6 Tbsp.	salt	100 mL
3½ cups	water	875 mL
1¼ cups	white vinegar	300 mL

1. Cut turnips in half, then into thin slices, about ⅛ inch (3 mm).
2. In 3 one-cup (250-mL) sterilized glass jars, pack the turnips tightly with garlic cloves, placing pieces of raw beet between the layers at regular intervals.
3. Dissolve salt in water and stir in vinegar. Cover the vegetables with this solution and seal the jars tightly.
4. Store in a warm place for 10 days to mellow and then transfer to a cool spot.
5. Label and attach Serving Suggestions.
Makes 3 cups (750 mL).

SERVING SUGGESTIONS
Serve as a relish with stews, curries and shish kebab. Keep refrigerated. Consume within 4–6 weeks.

Peach and Pepper Relish

12	large ripe peaches	12
6	sweet green peppers, finely chopped	6
6	sweet red peppers, finely chopped	6
1	small hot red pepper, finely chopped	1
1 cup	cider vinegar	250 mL
1 Tbsp.	coarse salt	15 mL
2	lemons, sliced	2
4 cups	white sugar	1 L

1. To remove skins from peaches, immerse fruit in boiling water for 2 minutes, then place in cold water for 30 seconds. Drain, skin, pit and cut into eighths.

2. Combine peaches, peppers, vinegar, salt and lemons in large saucepan and bring to a boil, stirring constantly. Reduce heat and simmer uncovered for 30 minutes. Remove lemon slices. Add sugar and simmer another 40 minutes or until mixture has a thick, relish consistency.

3. Ladle into sterilized jars, cool and refrigerate. Or ladle into 8 one-cup (250-mL) sterilized canning jars, leaving ⅛-inch (3-mm) headspace, and process for 15 minutes (see "About Canning," p. 120).

4. Label and attach Serving Suggestions. You might want to present a container of cream cheese with the Peach and Pepper Relish.

Makes 2 quarts (2 L).

SERVING SUGGESTIONS
Serve over cream cheese with heart-shaped lahvosh (kosher flatbread) biscuits or on toasted French bread slices. Delicious as a condiment with chicken, pork, duck or lamb. Keep refrigerated. Consume within 4–6 weeks.

Mom's Zucchini Relish

10 cups	chopped zucchini	2.5 L
4 cups	chopped onions	1 L
5 Tbsp.	salt	75 mL
1 tsp.	turmeric	5 mL
2¼ cups	white vinegar	550 mL
1 tsp.	nutmeg	5 mL
1 tsp.	dry mustard	5 mL
2 tsp.	celery seed	10 mL
1 Tbsp.	cornstarch	15 mL
4 cups	sugar	1 L
1	sweet red pepper, chopped	1
1	sweet green pepper, chopped	1
1 Tbsp.	hot red pepper, chopped	15 mL

1. Combine zucchini, onions and salt in a large glass or stainless steel bowl and let stand overnight at room temperature. Drain in a colander and rinse twice with cold water.

2. Combine with remaining ingredients in a saucepan and bring to a boil. Reduce heat and simmer uncovered, stirring often, for 30 minutes or until some of the liquid evaporates.

3. Let mixture cool. Ladle into sterilized jars, cool and store in the refrigerator.

4. If you prefer to preserve the relish by canning, ladle the boiling mixture into 6 or 7 two-cup (500-mL) sterilized canning jars, leaving ⅛-inch (3-mm) headspace, and process for 5 minutes (see "About Canning," p. 120).

5. Label and attach Serving Suggestions.
Makes 3–3½ quarts (3–3.5 L).

SERVING SUGGESTIONS
Serve with roasted meats, baked ham and open-faced sandwiches. Store refrigerated, keeps about a year.

Red River Relish

7	large cucumbers, peeled, seeded and finely chopped	7
5	large onions, finely chopped	5
2	sweet red peppers, finely chopped	2
2	sweet green peppers, finely chopped	2
¾ cup	pickling salt	175 mL
2½ cups	white sugar	625 mL
½ cup	all-purpose flour	125 mL
2 tsp.	turmeric powder	10 mL
1 Tbsp.	dry mustard	15 mL
1 Tbsp.	celery seed	15 mL
2 cups	white vinegar	500 mL
1 cup	water	250 mL

A specialty of the house in the home of the Joneses, my former Winnipeg neighbours.

1. Place cucumbers, onions and peppers in a bowl, sprinkle with pickling salt and toss well to mix. Cover with plastic wrap and refrigerate overnight. The next day, drain in a colander and rinse well.

2. Combine dry ingredients and add to 1 cup (250 mL) of vinegar and set aside.

3. Combine drained vegetables, water and remaining 1 cup (250 mL) vinegar in a large saucepan and boil for 5 minutes. Add vinegar solution and boil 5 minutes more or until clear. Immediately ladle into 8 two-cup (500-mL) sterilized canning jars, leaving about ¼-inch (6-mm) headspace, and process for 10 minutes (see "About Canning," p. 120.)

4. Label and attach Serving Suggestions.

Makes 2 quarts (2 L).

SERVING SUGGESTIONS

Delicious with frankfurters and hamburgers. Refrigerate after opening. Keeps about a year.

Onion and Cranberry Marmalade

*Grenadine, a red syrup with a
sweet-tart flavour, gives this
marmalade its attractive
pink colouring.*

2 Tbsp.	unsalted butter	25 mL
2 Tbsp.	olive oil	25 mL
8	medium onions, thinly sliced (about 3 lbs./1.4 kg)	8
1 tsp.	salt	5 mL
	freshly ground pepper	
½ cup	sugar	125 mL
⅓ cup	red wine vinegar	75 mL
¼ cup	grenadine syrup	50 mL
1 cup	dry red wine	250 mL
1 cup	fresh cranberries	250 mL

1. Melt butter and oil in a large skillet over medium-high heat. Add onions, salt, pepper and sugar and sauté for 10 minutes or until tender. Add vinegar, grenadine and wine and simmer covered for 45 minutes.

2. Add cranberries and continue to cook for 15 minutes or until reduced to a marmalade consistency.

3. Ladle into sterilized jars, cool and refrigerate.

4. Label and attach Serving Suggestions.

Makes 3 cups (750 mL).

SERVING SUGGESTIONS
An excellent accompaniment to roasted meats and poultry; or heat and serve warm with terrines, cold meats or breaded oysters. Keep refrigerated, consume within 4 weeks.

Gifts from the Pantry

Here is a collection of hors d'oeuvre,
pâtés, soups and utterly decadent treats,
for you to make and stash away
for the right person
at the right moment.
All the foods are complemented
by a variety of items you can buy,
mix and match in your gift package.

HORS D'OEUVRE TO GO

Next time you are invited to a party, make it complete by taking along an easily transportable hors d'oeuvre. Pack the Baked Garlic in the centre of an attractive covered cheese platter and arrange the Dill Toast Hearts around it. Or make Baked Garlic Dip and prepare a tray of crudités to accompany it.

Garlic Braid. If you are in a hurry and haven't had time to shop for a gift or to cook, give a gift of a braid of garlic and tie the recipes for Baked Garlic, Baked Garlic Dip and Dill Toast Hearts to the braid. Decorative garlic braids can be purchased in many different lengths. When buying them, insist on firm, plump heads.

Baked Garlic

1 lb.	garlic (about 10 heads)	500 g
3/4 cup	olive oil	175 mL
3 Tbsp.	fresh thyme	50 mL
3 Tbsp.	fresh basil	50 mL
	salt and freshly ground pepper	

1. Preheat oven to 300°F (150°C).
2. Peel off outer leaves from each head of garlic, keeping the head and inner leaves intact. Score each head of garlic about 1/3 inch (8 mm) from the top so that the cloves are exposed.
3. Combine oil and fresh herbs.
4. Place heads of garlic in a single layer in a baking dish that will just hold them. Sprinkle the oil and herb mixture, salt and pepper over the garlic.
5. Bake for approximately 1 hour or until garlic is very soft and tender. Serve whole heads of garlic. Slip the garlic cloves out of their skins and spread like butter on cream cheese or goat cheese on Dill Toast Hearts (recipe below) or make Baked Garlic Dip (recipe below).

Allow 1–2 heads per person.

Don't be alarmed at the amount of garlic called for in this recipe—you are in for a delicious surprise. Baked garlic is irresistible.

Baked Garlic Dip

⅓ lb.	Baked Garlic (3–4 heads)	150 g
½ lb.	Winnipeg-style cream cheese	250 g
2 Tbsp.	fresh dill, finely chopped (optional)	25 mL

Pinch garlic cloves from their skins into food processor. Add cream cheese and dill. Process using metal blade until puréed. Serve at room temperature with crudités.

Makes 1⅓ cups (325 mL).

Dill Toast Hearts

10 slices	day-old white bread	10 slices
6 Tbsp.	butter, softened	100 mL
2 Tbsp.	chopped fresh dill	25 mL

1. Preheat oven to 350°F (180°C).
2. To make toast hearts, remove crusts from bread and stamp out hearts with a 3-inch (7.5-cm) cookie cutter.
3. Combine butter and dill and spread on bread.
4. Arrange on a cookie sheet and bake for 10 minutes or until golden.

Allow 1–2 slices per person.

Carrot Artichoke Antipasto

¼ cup	olive oil	50 mL
2	medium carrots, sliced in rounds	2
2	medium green peppers, chopped	2
2	medium ribs celery, chopped	2
1 cup	tomato chili sauce	250 mL
1 cup	ketchup	250 mL
1 cup	baby gherkins	250 mL
1 cup	tiny pickled onions	250 mL
½ cup	stuffed olives	125 mL
½ cup	Greek olives	125 mL
7-oz. can	solid tuna, drained	198-g can
½ cup	apple cider vinegar	125 mL
2 14-oz. cans	artichoke hearts, cut in half	2 398-mL cans

1. In a large heavy saucepan, heat olive oil. Add carrots, green peppers and celery and sauté gently for 10 minutes.

2. Add chili sauce, ketchup, gherkins, onions and olives and simmer for 10 minutes, stirring occasionally.

3. Add tuna, breaking into large chunks. Stir in vinegar and add artichoke hearts. Simmer until heated through.

4. Transfer to 7 one-cup (250-mL) sterilized glass containers, cover, cool, label and refrigerate. Keeps for 1 week.

5. If you prefer to can the antipasto, ladle the hot mixture into 7 one-cup (250-mL) sterilized canning jars, leaving ¼-inch (6-mm) headspace, and process for 10 minutes (see "About Canning," p. 120). Label containers. Keeps about a year.

Makes 7 cups (1.75 L).

There are many variations for antipasto, but this is my favourite.

PERFECT PATES

Pâtés are savoury dishes to give alone or with a hearty bread, soup and dessert for an elegant light meal.

Stilton Pâté

8 oz.	cream cheese	250 g
2 Tbsp.	whipping cream	30 mL
8 oz.	Stilton cheese	250 g
2 Tbsp.	port	30 mL
2	small gherkins OR other sweet pickles, minced	2
4	stuffed green olives, minced	4
1 clove	garlic, minced	1 clove

1. Place cream cheese in a food processor with a metal blade. With machine running, add the cream. Add Stilton cheese and process until blended.

2. Add port, gherkins, olives and garlic and process until smooth.

3. Place in 2 one-cup (250-mL) crocks and chill.

4. Cover with lids or self-adhering plastic wrap, and refrigerate. Before presenting, add note: "Will keep for 2 weeks in refrigerator. Serve at room temperature."

Makes 1 pound (500 g).

Narsai's Duck Liver Pâté

1½ cups	butter	375 mL
1 cup	sliced onions	250 mL
1	green apple, peeled, cored and sliced	1
1 lb.	duck livers OR chicken livers, rinsed, dried and cut in half	500 g
¼ cup	applejack OR sherry	50 mL
¼ cup	whipping cream	50 mL
1¼ tsp.	salt	6 mL
1 tsp.	lemon juice	5 mL

I first tasted this pâté at a special celebration for Julia Child in San Francisco.

1. Melt ½ cup (125 mL) butter in a skillet. Add onions and sauté until they begin to brown. Add apple and cook 3 minutes or until soft. Add livers and sauté over high heat until pink inside. Transfer livers, onions and apple to a food processor with metal blade. Reserve pan residue.

2. Pour applejack onto pan residue in skillet and stir over high heat for 2 minutes, then add to liver mixture in food processor. Add cream. Process until smooth. Remove and cool to lukewarm.

3. Using electric mixer, beat 1 cup (250 mL) butter until soft and slowly add liver mixture. Add salt and lemon juice.

4. Pack pâté into a 4-cup (1-L) terrine or 4 one-cup (250-mL) small ceramic crocks and cover with a thin layer of melted butter or Port Wine Aspic (see below).

5. Cover with self-adhering plastic, label and refrigerate. Before presenting, add this note: "Pâté will keep 4 days in the refrigerator."

Makes 2 pounds (1 kg).

Port Wine Aspic

2 tsp.	gelatin	10 mL
1 cup	port	250 mL
2 Tbsp.	sugar	25 mL
1 Tbsp.	water	15 mL
3 Tbsp.	red wine vinegar	50 mL
½ tsp.	tarragon, crumbled	2 mL

1. Soften gelatin in ¼ cup (50 mL) port and set aside.

2. Dissolve sugar in water in small saucepan and cook rapidly over medium heat until sugar melts and reaches a medium-dark caramel colour. Add vinegar, ¾ cup (200 mL) port and tarragon, and simmer for 2 minutes.

3. Add gelatin solution to hot mixture and stir until dissolved.

4. Spoon through fine strainer over pâté in a terrine or crocks until ⅛ –¼ inch (3 –6 mm) thick, then chill until set.

Valentine's Day Variation includes Winnipeg Goldeye Pâté, Dill Toast Hearts, Petite Licorelle, fluted glasses and Boysenberry Truffles. Add roses and pack in a heart-shaped box.

Winnipeg Goldeye Pâté

1 lb.	Winnipeg goldeye, cut into 1-inch (2.5-cm) pieces	500 g
¼ cup	finely chopped red onions	50 mL
1 Tbsp.	finely chopped fresh dill	15 mL
3 Tbsp.	fresh lime juice	50 mL
¼ cup	mayonnaise	50 mL
1 cup	butter, melted	250 mL

1. Carefully pick over the goldeye to remove all traces of bone.

2. In a food processor with a metal blade, combine goldeye, onions, dill, lime juice and mayonnaise by turning machine on and off about 8 times.

3. Add melted butter and process the mixture for 1 minute or until puréed.

4. Spoon mixture into 2 one-cup (250-mL) crocks.

5. Cover with self-adhering plastic wrap, label and refrigerate. Before presenting, add a note to keep refrigerated and consume within 48 hours.

Makes 1 pound (500 g).

This extraordinary pâté is made with Winnipeg goldeye, an orange-gold fish delicacy that is soaked in brine and then smoked over burning oak wood. If you can't find it, use smoked coonie, a light whitefish smoked in Winnipeg.

Sweet Samplers: Congratulations can be offered in a decorative box filled with champagne, long-stemmed glasses, strawberries, Crème Fraîche and Black Beast (foreground).

A TUREEN OF SOUPS

Dinner in a Pot. Deliver Spicy Chorizo and Corn Chowder in a rustic bean pot accompanied by Buttermilk Corn Muffins (p. 57), a carafe of Karen's Creamy Caesar Dressing (p. 24) and a dessert. The cheese and chorizo garnishes may be packed in brightly coloured serviettes lined with plastic wrap and tied with a bow.

    Dinner in a Thermos. Deliver the Market Chowder in a large thermos with a loaf of Irish Wheaten Bread (p. 66), a crock of Maple Butter (p. 67) and Iced Double-Chocolate Cookies (p. 84).

Pumpkin Soup

This soup may be served hot or chilled in a pumpkin shell.

¼ cup	butter	50 mL
1 cup	minced white parts of leeks	250 mL
	OR green onions	
½ cup	chopped onions	125 mL
2 cups	canned pumpkin	500 mL
	OR steamed, puréed pumpkin	
4 cups	chicken broth	1 L
½ tsp.	curry powder	2 mL
1 tsp.	salt	5 mL
¼ tsp.	white pepper	1 mL
¼ tsp.	cinnamon	1 mL
¼ tsp.	nutmeg	1 mL
1	bay leaf	1
1 cup	whipping cream	250 mL

To make the steamed, puréed pumpkin called for in this recipe, scrape out seeds and pulp, peel and cut pumpkin into 2-inch (5-cm) chunks. Place pumpkin in a steamer basket over 1 inch (2.5 cm) boiling water and cover with a lid. Steam for 15–20 minutes, then purée. A 4-lb. (1.8 kg) pumpkin will yield 4 cups (1 L) steamed, puréed flesh.

1. In a soup pot, melt butter and sauté leeks and onions until tender. Add pumpkin, chicken broth and seasonings. Bring to a boil and simmer for 15 minutes. Remove the bay leaf.

2. Pour pumpkin mixture into a blender or food processor with a metal blade and purée until smooth. Return to soup pot, add whipping cream and cook over moderate heat, stirring occasionally until heated through. Adjust seasonings.

3. Pumpkin shells make excellent serving containers. Wash a 6–8 lb. (2.7–3.6 kg) pumpkin, cut out a lid, and scrape out seeds and pulp. Wipe out the inside. Brush inside with 2 Tbsp. (25 mL) melted butter and sprinkle with salt. Replace lid and bake in a 350°F (180°C) oven for 45 minutes. Add heated soup to pumpkin and serve. Or cool pumpkin and add chilled soup and serve. Scoop out a few small chunks of pumpkin from the shell to garnish the soup.

Makes about 1½ quarts (1.5 L).

The Market Chowder

This is one of the most popular recipes in my Granville Island Cookbook.

5 strips	bacon, diced	5 strips
1	onion, chopped	1
1 clove	garlic, crushed	1 clove
1	green pepper, thinly sliced	1
2	medium carrots, thinly sliced	2
2 Tbsp.	chopped parsley	25 mL
2 14-oz. cans	tomatoes, chopped	2 398-mL cans
2 10-oz. cans	clam nectar	2 284-mL cans
1 cup	dry red wine	250 mL
1 Tbsp.	fresh thyme OR	15 mL
½ tsp.	dried thyme	2 mL
	salt and freshly ground pepper	
2 cups	potatoes, peeled and diced	500 mL
8 oz.	salmon, cut into bite-sized pieces	250 g
8 oz.	scallops	250 g
6 oz.	crabmeat	170 g
6 oz.	shrimp	170 g

1. Sauté bacon in soup pot until crisp. Add onion, garlic, green pepper, carrots and parsley and cook over medium heat for 10 minutes, stirring occasionally.

2. Add tomatoes, clam nectar, red wine, thyme, salt and pepper and bring to a boil. Simmer covered for 20 minutes.

3. Add potatoes, cover and simmer a further 30 minutes until potatoes are tender.

4. Add salmon and cook for 5 minutes. Add scallops, crabmeat and shrimp and simmer for 5 more minutes. Do not overcook.

5. Transfer immediately to a thermos and cover to ensure that the chowder does not need reheating on arrival.

Makes 3 quarts (3 L).

Spicy Chorizo and Corn Chowder

Chorizo is a garlicky, spicy pork sausage.

8 oz.	chorizo, casings removed and crumbled, OR bacon, diced	250 g
2	large onions, chopped	2
1½ cups	chopped celery with tops	375 mL
2 4-oz. cans	green chilies, drained and diced	2 113-g cans
¼ tsp.	curry powder	1 mL
4 Tbsp.	all-purpose flour	60 mL
2 14-oz. cans	whole-kernel corn	2 398-mL cans
1 tsp.	salt	5 mL
¼ tsp.	white pepper	1 mL
3 cups	milk	750 mL
3 cups	light cream	750 mL
3 cups	shredded Monterey Jack cheese	750 mL

1. Brown chorizo in frying pan, remove, drain and set aside.
2. Using ⅓ cup (75 mL) of the remaining fat, sauté onions, celery and chilies for 10 minutes or until tender.
3. Blend in curry powder and flour. Add undrained corn, salt and pepper. Cook over low heat, stirring, until mixture is bubbling.
4. Remove from heat, stir in milk and cream. Return to low heat and cook until chowder simmers, stirring constantly until warmed through.
5. Transfer to gift pot and cover. Package chorizo and shredded cheese separately and enclose Serving Suggestions.
   Makes 2½ quarts (2.5 L).

SERVING SUGGESTIONS
Just before serving, add half the cheese. Serve in soup bowls garnished with remaining cheese and chorizo.

INDECENT INDULGENCES

When you really want to spoil someone, make one of these gifts.

Solitary Splendour. Sometimes less is more, and this is especially true when you have very little time and want to splurge on one or two lavish items rather than a collection of inexpensive ones. Fruit preserved in liqueur looks beautiful in any size of glass jar, so select an elegant glass or crystal container from a gift shop and make one of the combinations suggested in Fruit in Liqueur.

A Peck of Presents. If you want to dress up the Fruit in Liqueur, decorate the jar with an elegant bow and present it with glass dessert dishes and dessert spoons. The whole package will fit nicely into a farmer's market peck-sized fruit basket.

For winter enthusiasts to enjoy by the fireside, pack Frozen Cappuccino Mix and Liqueur Mix or a mugful of Hot Buttered Rum Mix with an old-fashioned spattered blue and white metal coffeepot, basin or large kettle. To either gift add a deck of cards or the latest game. Or tie cinnamon sticks to the handle of the mug of Hot Buttered Rum Mix, and include a small bottle of dark rum, a nutmeg grater and whole nutmeg. With the Frozen Cappuccino Mix, tuck in a small bottle of Liqueur Mix and a small bag of chocolate-covered coffee beans.

Sundae Kit Deluxe. Present Amaretto Praline Sauce in an old-fashioned sundae glass, or in an ice cream tub. Add a jar of homemade Praline and pack with your favourite ice cream in a styrofoam cooler to which you have added an ice pack. Before you close the lid, add a European chocolate bar to grate onto the sundaes, and perhaps a calorie counter, a dressmaker's tape measure, some elegant gold doilies and two parfait spoons.

Boysenberry Truffles

½ lb.	chocolate	250 g
4 Tbsp.	butter	60 mL
½ cup	seedless boysenberry jam	125 mL
½ cup	chopped almonds	125 mL
2 Tbsp.	framboise liqueur	25 mL
½ cup	sifted imported Dutch cocoa	125 mL

1. Melt chocolate and butter in a double boiler over hot water and stir till smooth. Add jam, almonds and liqueur and combine thoroughly. Place in a bowl and refrigerate until firm.

2. Using a melon baller or spoon, mould into 1-inch (2.5-cm) balls. They should look uneven. Roll balls in cocoa and place in foil bonbon cups.

3. Store in refrigerator or freezer. Before presenting, label and note: "Refrigerate until served."

Makes 24 truffles.

Praline

Praline is a delicious crunchy combination of caramelized nuts.

2 cups	walnuts, pecans, hazelnuts OR blanched almonds	500 mL
2 cups	sugar	500 mL
¼ cup	water	50 mL
	butter	

1. Preheat oven to 350°F (180°C).
2. Toast nuts on an ungreased baking sheet in oven for 12 minutes or until lightly browned, stirring frequently. Set aside.
3. In a heavy saucepan, combine sugar and water over medium-high heat and bring to a boil without stirring, swirling the pan occasionally. When the syrup is golden brown and caramelized, remove the pan from the heat and stir in the nuts.
4. Pour onto a buttered baking sheet and cool completely.
5. Turn into a plastic bag that has plenty of extra room. Tie bag and crush praline with a wooden mallet until there is a mixture of small pieces and crumbs.
6. Set aside 1 cup to make Amaretto Praline Sauce. Spoon remainder into two one-cup (250-mL) jars, cover, label and attach Serving Suggestions. One jar should accompany Amaretto Praline Sauce (recipe below). Reserve the other jar for future use.

Makes 3 cups (750 mL).

SERVING SUGGESTIONS
Delicious in salads, mousses and custards or sprinkled on ice cream and cakes; or with Amaretto Praline Sauce.

Amaretto Praline Sauce

1 lb.	white chocolate	500 g
6 Tbsp.	butter	100 mL
1 cup	boiling water	250 mL
¾ cup	corn syrup	200 mL
½ cup	amaretto liqueur	125 mL
1 cup	Praline, crushed in food processor	250 mL

A rich confection made with white chocolate.

1. Melt ½ lb. (250 g) white chocolate and butter in top of double boiler over hot water. Transfer to a heavy saucepan, add boiling water and corn syrup and stir well over low heat until mixture starts to boil. Allow the sauce to boil without stirring for 8 minutes.

2. Remove the sauce from the heat and add the remaining ½ lb. (250 g) white chocolate. Cool, add amaretto and Praline and refrigerate.

3. Pack in 3 old-fashioned sundae glasses or one-cup (250-mL) ice cream tubs. Cover tops of glasses with self-adhering plastic wrap, label and attach Serving Suggestion.

Makes about 3 cups (750 mL).

SERVING SUGGESTION
Serve warm over ice cream with grated chocolate and Praline.

Frozen Cappuccino Mix

¼ cup	sugar	50 mL
⅓ cup	water	75 mL
2 oz.	unsweetened chocolate	60 g
1 oz.	semisweet chocolate	30 g
2	egg yolks	2
3 Tbsp.	brandy	50 mL
3 cups	whipping cream	750 mL
⅓ cup	instant espresso coffee powder	75 mL

1. In a small saucepan, bring sugar and water to a boil over moderate heat. Boil for 3 minutes.

2. In a food processor with a metal blade, chop chocolate. With motor running, pour hot sugar syrup through feeder tube and process for 10 seconds. Add egg yolks and process for 10 seconds. Add brandy. Mix well.

3. In mixing bowl, whip cream with espresso powder until thick. Add the chocolate mixture and mix well. Line 6 mugs with plastic sandwich bags, pour the mix into lined mugs, cover and label. Store in freezer.

Makes 1½ quarts (1.5 L).

Liqueur Mix

⅓ cup	dark rum	75 mL
¾ cup	amaretto liqueur	175 mL
1 cup	Kahlua	250 mL

1. Mix all ingredients and pour into 2 clean one-cup (250-mL) recycled piccolo champagne bottles.
2. Cap or cork, label and attach Serving Suggestions.
Makes 1 pint (500 mL).

SERVING SUGGESTIONS
Add 1 heaping Tbsp. (15 mL) of Frozen Cappuccino Mix and ½–1 ounce (15–30 mL) Liqueur Mix to a cup of hot coffee. Stir well. Top with a dollop of whipping cream if desired.

Fruit in Liqueur

14-oz. can	fruit, drained	398-mL can
¾ cup	syrup from fruit	175 mL
¾ cup	liqueur	175 mL

1. Drain canned fruit, reserving the syrup, and place in 2 one-cup (250-mL) sterilized glass jars.
2. Combine strained canning syrup and the appropriate liqueur, mixed half-and-half. Pour over fruit to cover; seal.
3. Label your gift with its name and a note to store in refrigerator. Keeps 4 weeks.
Makes 2¼ cups (550 mL).

Use one of the following combinations of canned fruit and liqueur: peaches in brandy, apricots in apricot brandy, pears in crème de menthe, cherries in Kirsch, mandarin oranges in Cointreau, or a mix of several fruits in brandy. The longer these stand, the better they taste.

Hot Buttered Rum Mix

½ lb.	butter at room temperature	250 g
1 lb.	brown sugar	500 g
1 lb.	icing sugar	500 g
2	eggs	2
1 tsp.	vanilla	5 mL
1 qt.	vanilla ice cream, softened	1 L
½ tsp.	nutmeg	2 mL
½ tsp.	cinnamon	2 mL
½ tsp.	cloves	2 mL

1. In a mixing bowl, cream butter and add brown sugar, icing sugar, eggs and vanilla. Add ice cream and spices and combine thoroughly.

2. Line 8 mugs with plastic sandwich bags, add the batter to the lined mugs, label and tie with a ribbon at the top. Store in freezer. Before presenting, attach Serving Suggestions.

Makes 2 quarts (2 L).

SERVING SUGGESTIONS
Place 1 heaping Tbsp. (15 mL) of mix into cup or mug. Add 1½ oz. (45 mL) of dark rum. Add boiling water to fill and stir to blend. Serve with cinnamon stick, if desired. Children love this without the rum! Store in refrigerator or freezer.

Gifts from the Oven

Desserts, fancy breads and butters,
and designer snacks —
all make excellent gifts
on their own or in combination.
You can present an assortment
of delicious cakes and cookies
elegantly arranged as a gift platter.

BREADS AND BUTTERS

Bake a batch of breads to give away by themselves or with creamy butters. Set aside an afternoon for baking; while one batch is in the oven, wrap what you baked earlier.

Brie-Box Gift. Wrap several loaves in clear plastic wrap and place them in the cover or base of a Brie box from your local cheese store. Add Maple Butter to a loaf of Irish Wheaten Bread; a crock of White Chocolate Butter to a Strawberry Loaf, or a round of goat cheese or Bell Pepper Butter to Parmesan Herbed Bread.

Breadbasket Gift. Line a French breadbasket with colourful tissue paper and add Parmesan Herbed Bread, a pepper plant and a red or green bell pepper filled with Bell Pepper Butter.

Irish Wheaten Bread

3 cups	stone-ground wholewheat flour	750 mL
3 cups	all-purpose flour	750 mL
1½ tsp.	salt	7 mL
3 Tbsp.	sugar	50 mL
5 tsp.	baking powder	20 mL
1½ tsp.	baking soda	7 mL
1 cup	butter, chilled	250 mL
3 cups	buttermilk	750 mL

1. Preheat oven to 375°F (190°C).
2. In a mixing bowl, combine flour, salt, sugar, baking powder and baking soda. Cut in butter until mixture resem-

bles coarse crumbs. Make a well in the centre of the flour mixture and add buttermilk, stirring until blended.

3. Knead dough until it is in one piece, then knead 12 times.

4. Cut dough in half and shape into two round loaves. Place in greased 8-inch (1.2-L) round cake tins.

5. Bake for 1 hour or until bread sounds hollow when tapped. Let bread cool on wire rack until set.

6. Wrap in plastic wrap, label and present with Maple Butter and Serving Suggestions.

Makes 2 loaves.

SERVING SUGGESTIONS

Cut Irish Wheaten Bread into thin slices. Delicious toasted; or broil for a few seconds with cheddar cheese on top. Also good with Maple Butter.

Maple Butter

¼ lb.	unsalted butter at room temperature	125 g
1 cup	maple syrup	250 mL
1 Tbsp.	maple syrup liqueur OR	15 mL
1 tsp.	maple flavouring	5 mL

1. In a mixing bowl, cream butter, add maple syrup and liqueur until mixture is smooth and creamy.

2. Spoon into 2 one-cup (250-mL) crocks or miniature 4-oz. (125-mL) soufflé dishes. Wrap airtight, label and refrigerate.

Makes 2 cups (500 mL).

Parmesan Herbed Bread

2½ cups	all-purpose flour	625 mL
2 Tbsp.	sugar	30 mL
1 Tbsp.	baking powder	15 mL
½ tsp.	baking soda	3 mL
¼ tsp.	dry mustard	1 mL
¼ tsp.	salt	1 mL
¼ tsp.	pepper	1 mL
¼ tsp.	cayenne pepper	1 mL
1 Tbsp.	chopped fresh oregano	15 mL
1¼ cups	freshly grated Parmesan cheese	300 mL
⅓ cup	chopped fresh parsley	80 mL
⅓ cup	olive oil	80 mL
2	eggs, lightly beaten	2
1½ cups	buttermilk	375 mL

1. Heat oven to 350°F (180°C).

2. In a large mixing bowl, combine flour, sugar, baking powder, baking soda, mustard, salt, pepper and cayenne pepper. Stir in oregano, 1 cup (250 mL) of Parmesan and parsley.

3. In a small mixing bowl, combine oil, eggs and buttermilk and stir well.

4. Make a well in the centre of the dry ingredients and add liquid mixture all at once. Mix lightly until ingredients are just blended. Spread batter evenly into a greased 9 × 5-inch (2-L) prepared loaf pan.

5. Bake for 40 minutes. Sprinkle with remaining Parmesan and bake an additional 5 minutes or until metal skewer inserted at centre comes out clean.

6. Cool in pan for 10 minutes, then remove from pan and finish cooling on a rack.

7. Wrap in plastic wrap, label and present with Bell Pepper Butter or goat cheese and Serving Suggestion.

Makes 1 loaf.

SERVING SUGGESTION

Serve with Bell Pepper Butter. Wonderful with goat cheese.

Bell Pepper Butter

2	sweet red peppers	2
½ lb.	unsalted butter, at room temperature	250 g

For a colourful touch of the South, serve this butter in a red pepper.

1. Seed and cut 1 pepper into eighths and place with butter in a food processor with a metal blade. Process until smooth.

2. Cut top off remaining pepper and seed it. Scoop butter into pepper and replace top.

3. Cover pepper with plastic wrap, label and refrigerate.

4. Before presenting, attach Serving Suggestions.

Makes ½ pound (250 g).

SERVING SUGGESTIONS

Serve with Parmesan Herbed Bread or corn on the cob.

Strawberry Loaf

Strawberries do not ripen after they are picked, so refrigerate them as quickly as possible. Rinse them just before you want to use them; keep the stems on while rinsing to prevent water from diluting the flavour and changing the texture.

½ cup	butter	125 mL
1 cup	sugar	250 mL
½ tsp.	almond extract	2 mL
2	eggs, separated	2
2 cups	all-purpose flour	500 mL
1 tsp.	baking powder	5 mL
1 tsp.	baking soda	5 mL
1 tsp.	cinnamon	5 mL
1 tsp.	salt	5 mL
1 cup	chopped fresh strawberries OR	250 mL

frozen strawberries, drained (reserve juice to make Strawberry Spread, recipe below)

1. Preheat oven to 350°F (180°C).
2. In a mixing bowl cream butter, sugar and almond extract. Beat in egg yolks.
3. Sift together flour, baking powder, baking soda, cinnamon and salt. Add the dry ingredients alternately with strawberries to mixing bowl.
4. Beat egg whites until stiff. Fold into mixture.
5. Line a 9 × 5-inch (2-L) pan with greased wax paper. Pour batter into pan and bake 50 minutes or until metal skewer inserted at centre comes out clean. Cool in pan for 10 minutes, then remove from pan and cool on a wire rack.
6. Wrap in plastic wrap, label and present with White Chocolate Butter or Strawberry Spread and Serving Suggestions.

Makes 1 loaf.

SERVING SUGGESTIONS
Serve Strawberry Loaf with White Chocolate Butter or Strawberry Spread. This bread freezes well and makes delicious toast on the second day after baking or thawing.

Strawberry Spread

8 oz.	cream cheese at room temperature	250 g
	syrup from frozen strawberries	

In a food processor with a metal blade, combine cream cheese with just enough syrup to make a spreadable mixture. Blend until smooth. Spoon into a crock, wrap airtight, label and refrigerate.
    Makes 1 cup (250 g).

If you use frozen fruit to make Strawberry Loaf, reserve the drained liquid and present the bread with this spread.

White Chocolate Butter

1¾ cup	icing sugar	425 mL
¼ lb.	unsalted butter at room temperature, cut into 4 pieces	125 g
1 Tbsp.	amaretto liqueur	15 mL
2 oz.	white chocolate, melted	60 g

1. In a food processor with a metal blade, process icing sugar to remove lumps. Add butter and amaretto to processor and process for 60 seconds or until smooth and creamy. Add white chocolate and process until thoroughly mixed, stopping to scrape down sides of bowl. Spoon into 2 one-cup (250-mL) crocks, wrap airtight, label and refrigerate.
    Makes 2 cups (500 mL).

DESSERT SAMPLER

Popular in European and North American restaurants, dessert samplers present an array of delectable combinations instead of just one dessert. These platters of sweets are often variations on a theme. Your selection of desserts may include exotic tropical fruits, sorbets or your favourite cheesecake baked in individual muffin cups. You could present a sampler of chocolate desserts, or combine chocolate items with lemon ones such as Citrus Fruit Bread Pudding. Simply place representative amounts of each dessert on an elegant serving tray.

Black Beast Box. You can show off the elegance of a chocolate and raspberry theme using a clear plastic flower box from the florist. Line the bottom of the box with pale pink tissue paper. Add Black Beast, raspberries in a tissue-lined basket, white chocolate truffles from your favourite *chocolatier,* and a small glass container of Crème Fraîche. Deliver it with a bottle of California Cabernet Sauvignon if you wish.

Pecan Cooler. Combine in a styrofoam cooler a French Pecan Tart and Praline, accompanied by a refreshing sorbet from your local ice cream parlour, a container of Crème Fraîche and an ice cream scoop.

Chocolate to Go. Chocolate-Covered Fortune Cookies shine when packaged in Chinese-food take-out containers lined with coloured tissue paper. Add some elegant lacquered chopsticks and a decorative container of green tea and present in a brown paper bag. You will find beautiful hand-decorated cards to accompany your gift in local Chinese shops.

Black Beast

1⅓ cups	sugar	325 mL
½ cup	water	125 mL
8 oz.	unsweetened chocolate	230 g
4 oz.	semisweet chocolate	115 g
8 oz.	unsalted butter at room temperature, cut in small pieces	230 g
5	eggs	5

This delicate chocolate confection from the Napa Valley in California is more like a cheesecake than a cake and is best served at room temperature. It is well worth the effort.

1. Preheat oven to 350°F (180°C).
2. Half-fill with hot water a roasting pan large enough to hold cake pan easily. Place on rack in lower third of oven.
3. Combine 1 cup (250 mL) sugar and water in small saucepan over medium-high heat and boil rapidly for 1 minute. Remove from heat and add chocolate, stirring until it is melted. Add butter piece by piece, beating with a wooden spoon until incorporated.
4. Beat eggs with rest of sugar until thick. Combine eggs with chocolate. Pour into a 9-inch-square (2.5-L) cake pan, greased and lined on the bottom with greased wax paper.
5. Place cake pan into roasting pan in oven. Bake for approximately 45 minutes or until top is dry and firm. Turn off oven, open oven door slightly and let cake sit for 20 minutes in oven. Remove from oven and let sit a further 20 minutes in the water bath, then unmould and sprinkle with icing sugar.
6. Present with a jar of Crème Fraîche (p. 75), on their own or in a dessert sampler, and Serving Suggestion.
   Serves 8–10.

SERVING SUGGESTION
Because it is so delicate, Black Beast may not cut neatly like a cake. Cut into squares or diamond shapes and serve with Crème Fraîche.

French Pecan Tart

My favourite pecan tart recipe is from Lydie Marshall, proprietor of A la Bonne Cocotte *(At the Good Cooking Pot) Cooking School in New York. Her unusual filling contains whipped cream that is baked with pecans and sugar.*

CREAM CHEESE PASTRY

1 cup	butter	250 mL
8 oz.	cream cheese	250 g
2 cups	all-purpose flour	500 g
1 dash	salt	1 dash
1 tsp.	grated lemon peel	5 mL
	dry beans to fill pastry shell	

1. Preheat oven to 400°F (200°C).
2. Blend butter, cream cheese, flour, salt and lemon peel with pastry blender or in food processor with metal blade. Chill about 1 hour.
3. Form dough into ball. Press evenly in a tart pan or pie plate about 11 inches (28 cm) in diameter. Trim the edges. Prick with fork and place in freezer for 20 minutes.
4. Remove tart crust from freezer and line it with foil. Fill with dry beans and prebake for 15 minutes. Remove foil and beans and cool crust.

PECAN FILLING

2 cups	pecans	500 mL
1 cup	whipping cream	250 mL
½ cup	sugar	125 mL

1. Grind pecans in a food processor with a metal blade until medium-fine.
2. With an electric beater, whip cream until firm, adding sugar gradually.
3. With a rubber spatula, fold in the pecans.
4. Fill the prebaked crust and place on a baking sheet. Bake in oven for 30 minutes. Remove the tart from the oven; it will set further as it cools.

5. Present this gift with a container of Crème Fraîche, on their own or in a dessert sampler. Include Serving Suggestion.

SERVING SUGGESTION
Serve with Crème Fraîche or whipped cream.

Crème Fraîche

1 cup	sour cream	250 mL
2 cups	whipping cream	500 mL
1 Tbsp.	fresh lemon juice	15 mL

1. Put the sour cream in a large mixing bowl. Slowly whisk in the whipping cream until thoroughly mixed. Cover with plastic wrap and put in a warm place for 8–24 hours or until the mixture has thickened.

2. Place a plastic coffee filter holder in a mixing bowl and insert a coffee filter paper. Pour the thickened cream mixture into the filter. Cover with plastic wrap, refrigerate and drain for 24–36 hours.

3. Stir lemon juice into thickened cream.

4. Pack in a set of crystal or antique-glass cream and sugar containers covered tightly with plastic wrap and refrigerate. Present with Black Beast or French Pecan Tart and include Serving Suggestions.

Makes 2 cups (500 mL).

SERVING SUGGESTIONS
This very thick cream is delicious served over fresh fruits and baked desserts. It keeps 4 weeks in the refrigerator.

Citrus Fruit Bread Pudding

6	lemons	6
3	limes	3
3	oranges	3
¾ cup	sugar	175 mL
2 cups	water	500 mL
8	croissants	8
	butter	

1. Zest rinds of lemons, limes and oranges in long, thin strips.
2. Section peeled oranges by cutting along the side of each dividing membrane to the core and lifting out segments from centre. Set aside.
3. Combine sugar and water in a small saucepan, bring to a boil, reduce heat and simmer for 5 minutes.
4. Butter one side of croissants, cut in quarters and press into a lightly buttered 8-cup (2-L) pudding mould or baking dish. Layer citrus rinds and orange sections over croissants. Pour syrup over all and refrigerate.
Serves 8.

SERVING SUGGESTION
Preheat oven to 300°F (150°C). Place mould in a shallow baking pan and fill pan half-way with hot water. Bake for 1 hour. Remove from water bath, cool 10 minutes and unmould pudding. Serve with Crème Fraîche (p. 75).

Italian Pasta Basket is packed inside a violin case. In the case are malfade, Chianti, olive oil, Pesto Cream Sauce, a cassette tape, a corkscrew, a sprig of oregano, garlic heads and a pasta fork. In front are Italian bread, black olives, Parmesan cheese and grapes. The tin at the back contains amaretti cookies.

Peach Fruitcake

1 cup	butter	250 mL
1½ cups	sugar	375 mL
5	eggs	5
2½ cups	drained preserved peaches OR	625 mL
19-oz. can	peaches, drained	540-mL can
3 cups	unbleached flour	750 mL
1 tsp.	baking powder	5 mL
½ tsp.	salt	2 mL
3 cups	raisins	750 mL
1 lb.	red and green cherries	450 g
1 cup	coconut	250 g
16	dried apricots	16
½ lb.	candied pineapple	250 g
2 tsp.	vanilla	10 mL
3–4 Tbsp.	brandy	50–60 mL

1. Preheat oven to 275°F (140°C).
2. In a mixing bowl, cream butter and sugar, add eggs one at a time, beating after each addition. Purée peaches and add. Beat in dry ingredients gradually. Lastly, fold in remaining fruit and flavouring.
3. Pour into several small loaf pans or several 10-ounce (300 mL) glass custard cups. Bake in oven for approximately 3 hours. Cool.

Makes two 9 by 5-inch (2 L) loaves.

Chinese Cooking Made Easy: The steamer contains ginger jars of Black Bean Sauce and Sesame Seed Sauce, with a jar of Szechuan Sauce in front; also in the basket are Chinese tea, water chestnuts and garlic chives; in front of the steamer are fortune cookies, egg noodles, soy sauce dishes and two Chinese melons.

Iced Rum Cake

Rum cake is traditionally a Christmas cake, but it is also a welcome addition to a dessert buffet any time of the year. Make it ahead, freeze it and spread Rum Icing on cake the same day you present your gift.

1 lb.	dates, chopped finely	500 g
1½ cups	brown sugar	375 g
1 cup	chopped walnuts	250 mL
½ tsp.	vanilla	2 mL
1 tsp.	cinnamon	5 mL
1 tsp.	salt	5 mL
¾ cup	butter	175 mL
1 tsp.	baking soda, dissolved in	5 mL
1 cup	boiling water	250 mL
2	eggs, well beaten	2
1 cup	sifted all-purpose flour	250 mL
2 Tbsp.	dark rum	25 mL

1. Preheat oven to 325°F (160°C).
2. Combine dates, sugar, walnuts, vanilla, cinnamon, salt and butter in a large mixing bowl and pour dissolved baking soda over all.
3. Combine eggs and flour thoroughly and add to mixture. It will be very thin.
4. Grease and line a 9-inch (3-L) angel-food or tube pan with waxed paper and add the batter.
5. Bake 1–1½ hours. Turn out of pan onto wire rack and drizzle dark rum over the top. When completely cool, add Rum Icing.
6. Present whole cake or cut into squares and combine with other sweets in a sampler, cookie jar or tin.

RUM ICING

4 oz.	butter	125 g
2 cups	sifted icing sugar	500 mL
2 Tbsp.	dark rum	25 mL
	light cream (optional)	

Using an electric hand mixer, beat butter, icing sugar and rum until fluffy. Thin with cream if necessary.

LEMON EGGNOG SAUCE

1 Tbsp.	sugar	15 mL
1 Tbsp.	cornstarch	15 mL
2 cups	eggnog	500 mL
	zest of 1 lemon	
2 Tbsp.	brandy	25 mL

1. In small saucepan, combine sugar and cornstarch. Gradually add eggnog and cook over medium heat, stirring constantly, till mixture thickens. Boil 2 minutes.

2. Remove from heat and add lemon zest and brandy.

3. Transfer to 2 Irish Coffee glasses and place plastic wrap on surface to prevent film. Additional eggnog may be added after chilling, for desired consistency.

4. Wrap tightly in plastic wrap, label and present with Iced Rum Cake and Serving Suggestions.

Makes 2 cups (500 mL).

SERVING SUGGESTIONS

Serve sauce chilled or warmed. Delicious on Iced Rum Cake, your favourite plum or carrot pudding and mince tarts.

Chocolate-Covered Fortune Cookies

Buy fortune cookies and dip them to give away, or if you have the time and patience, surprise your friends with homemade fortune cookies. Before you begin, write fortunes on 2-inch by ½-inch (5-cm by 1.3-cm) strips of paper.

2	eggs	2
⅓ cup	sugar	75 mL
¼ cup	vegetable oil	50 mL
½ cup	sifted all-purpose flour	125 mL
1½ Tbsp.	cornstarch	25 mL
¼ tsp.	salt	1 mL
¼ tsp.	ginger	1 mL
¼ tsp.	almond extract	1 mL
1¼ lb.	semisweet chocolate OR chocolate of your choice	600 g

1. In a small mixing bowl, beat eggs until light. Gradually add sugar, beating constantly. Beat in oil until mixture is well blended.

2. Sift together flour, cornstarch, salt and ginger and gradually fold into egg mixture. Add almond extract and blend.

3. Preheat electric skillet to 300°F (150°C) and grease lightly with oil. Drop batter into skillet by the tablespoon (15-mL spoon), spreading batter into a thin circle 3½–4 inches (9–10 cm) in diameter. Allow only 4 cookies at once in a 10-inch (25-cm) skillet.

4. Bake one side 5 minutes or until dry and lightly browned. Gently lift up cookies with pancake turner and turn. Bake on other side about 3 minutes.

5. Remove cookie from skillet. Quickly place fortune across centre and fold cookie in half away from you, bringing edges together until touching. Then bend the points of the half-circle toward each other. Cool cookies on rack or in a muffin tin.

6. Temper chocolate as in "About Tempering Chocolate," p. 122.

7. Dip half of each fortune cookie in tempered chocolate. Let excess chocolate drip back into pan.

8. Place cookies on wire rack over waxed paper to cool and harden.

Makes 20 cookies.

Iced Double-Chocolate Cookies

½ cup	butter, softened	125 mL
1 cup	sugar	250 mL
1	egg	1
2 oz.	unsweetened chocolate, melted	60 g
½ cup	plain yogurt	125 mL
1 tsp.	vanilla	5 mL
1¾ cup	self-raising flour	425 mL
½ cup	chopped walnuts	125 mL
1 cup	chocolate chips	250 mL

1. Preheat oven to 375°F (190°C).
2. In a mixing bowl, cream butter and sugar. Stir in egg, chocolate, yogurt and vanilla. Add flour, walnuts and chocolate chips and stir until ingredients are thoroughly combined. Chill for 1 hour.
3. Drop from teaspoon (5-mL spoon) onto a lightly greased baking sheet. Bake about 10 minutes. Remove from baking sheet, cool and spread with Mocha Icing.

Makes 36 cookies.

MOCHA ICING

¼ cup	butter	50 mL
2 Tbsp.	cocoa	25 mL
2 tsp.	instant coffee powder	10 mL
2 cups	sifted icing sugar	500 mL
1½ tsp.	vanilla	7 mL
3–4 Tbsp.	hot water	50–60 mL

Cream butter, cocoa and coffee powder. Beat in icing sugar, vanilla and hot water until mixture reaches spreading consistency. Spread on Double-Chocolate Cookies and let stand to set. Place cookies in paper muffin liners.

DESIGNER SNACKS

Fill beautiful tins to the brim with assorted designer snacks packed in cellophane bags. Or place the bags in a fancy shopping bag, a fireman's hat, a lunch kit, a sand pail, a straw wastebasket or a toy supermarket cart.

Mixed Curry Treat

4 qts.	popped popcorn, warm	4 L
2½ cups	unblanched raw almonds	625 mL
½ cup	butter, melted	125 mL
2 Tbsp.	curry powder	25 mL
1 tsp.	Tabasco sauce	5 mL
	salt	
2½ cups	raisins	625 mL

1. Preheat oven to 300°F (150°C).
2. Place warm popcorn and almonds in a large roasting pan. Combine butter, curry powder and Tabasco sauce and drizzle over popcorn mixture, tossing to coat evenly.
3. Bake in oven for 30 minutes, tossing every 10 minutes. Remove from oven and season with salt to taste.
4. Cool and store in airtight containers overnight to mellow flavours. Add raisins, pack in cellophane bags and label.
   Makes 4 quarts (4 L).

Oriental Popcorn

2 cups	chow mein noodles	500 mL
1 cup	unsalted roasted peanuts	250 mL
5 qts.	popped popcorn	5 L
⅔ cup	oil	150 mL
¼ cup	soy sauce	50 mL
1 Tbsp.	five-spice powder	15 mL
2 tsp.	garlic powder	10 mL
1 tsp.	salt	5 mL
1 tsp.	ground ginger	5 mL
1 tsp.	cayenne pepper	5 mL
2 Tbsp.	sesame seeds	25 mL

1. Heat oven to 300°F (150°C).
2. Pour popcorn, noodles and peanuts into a large roasting pan and place in oven until warm.
3. Combine rest of ingredients and mix thoroughly. Pour over popcorn mixture and toss to blend.
4. Bake in oven about 20 minutes, tossing 2 or 3 times. Cool and pack in cellophane bags and label.

Makes 5 quarts (5 L).

Homemade Crackerjacks

½ cup	brown sugar	125 mL
¼ cup	butter	50 mL
2 Tbsp.	dark corn syrup	25 mL
¼ tsp.	salt	1 mL
1 Tbsp.	molasses	15 mL
¼ tsp.	baking soda	1 mL
2 qts.	popped popcorn	2 L
½ cup	salted roasted peanuts	125 mL

1. Preheat oven to 250°F (120°C).
2. In a saucepan, combine brown sugar, butter, corn syrup, salt and molasses and bring to a boil. Reduce heat and simmer for 3 minutes. Remove from heat, add soda and stir until creamy.
3. Pour over popcorn, stirring to coat, and add peanuts. Spread on lightly greased jelly-roll pan and bake for 30 minutes. Cool and break into pieces, pack in cellophane bags and label.

Makes 2 quarts (2 L).

Chocolate-Dipped Potato Chips, Pretzels and Popcorn

ridged potato chips
pretzels
popped popcorn
1¼ lbs.   semisweet chocolate OR   600 g
chocolate of your choice

1. For best results, see "About Tempering Chocolate," p. 122. Dip unbroken potato chips and whole pretzels into chocolate, covering half of each piece. Let excess chocolate drip back into pan. In a large bowl, mix remaining chocolate and popcorn.

2. Place chocolate-coated pieces on wire racks over waxed paper to cool and harden.

3. Pack in cellophane bags and label.

Yield varies.

Gifts for Dinner

For that very special occasion
your gift can be an entire meal.
Simply provide the homemade
and store-bought basic ingredients,
then attach the instructions
and easy-to-follow recipes.
Choose from Italian, Chinese,
Southern, Southeast Asian
and West Coast menus.

ITALIAN PASTA BASKET

Pack a four-bottle wine basket or any other wicker basket with a jar of Carrot Artichoke Antipasto (p. 47), Pesto Cream Sauce, garlic butter, a loaf of crusty bread, a wedge of Parmesan cheese, *malfade* (narrow, ripple-edged pasta), Chianti and a package of amaretti cookies. Place the homemade Pesto Cream Sauce in a small glass container and garlic butter in a covered crock. Tie the malfade at the centre with a red ribbon.

You may also want to add one of the following: a red-checkered tablecloth, a Pavarotti or Verdi cassette, a cheese mill, a basil plant, candles and a wooden pasta fork.

Wrap the entire basket in clear cellophane and tie with red, green and white ribbon. Or call this gift the St. Valentine's Day Pastacre and place everything in a violin case; or simply add a water pistol!

Pesto Cream Sauce

1 cup	firmly packed fresh basil leaves	250 mL
8 oz.	cream cheese	250 g
2 Tbsp.	coarsely chopped fresh parsley leaves	30 mL
1 Tbsp.	coarsely shredded fresh mint leaves	15 mL
½ cup	olive oil	125 mL
½ cup	freshly grated Parmesan cheese OR	125 mL
¼ cup	each Parmesan and Romano cheese	50 mL
	salt and freshly ground pepper to taste	
½ cup	light cream	125 mL
½ cup	pine nuts OR walnuts (optional)	125 mL

1. In a food processor with a metal blade, combine basil, cream cheese, parsley and mint and blend thoroughly while gradually pouring oil through feeder tube. Add cheese, salt and pepper and process well. Add cream and blend thoroughly. Fold in pine nuts.

2. Pour into a jar, label and refrigerate.
Makes 2½ cups (625 mL).

SERVING SUGGESTION
Store in refrigerator. Keeps 2 weeks. Bring to room temperature and toss with cooked pasta to coat thoroughly.

CHINESE COOKING MADE EASY

Treat your friends to a Chinese dinner by preparing these sauces from recipes given to me by my friend Tony Vong of the popular Vong's Kitchen in Vancouver. All the ingredients may be obtained at Chinese and Asian food stores. Pack one or more of the sauces in ginger jars or unique glass bottles, together with the recipes for using each of the sauces.

These sauces will keep two weeks in the refrigerator or may be frozen for several months.

Your gift package might also contain egg noodles, jasmine tea, fortune cookies and lychees. You may want to add ivory chopsticks and painted Chinese bowls. Pack everything in a bamboo steamer or wok.

Sesame Seed Sauce

Sesame seed paste is made of toasted and ground sesame seeds and is similar to peanut butter, except that it has a claylike consistency.

3 Tbsp.	vegetable OR peanut oil	50 mL
4	medium garlic cloves, finely chopped	4
½ tsp.	dried whole red chilies, chopped	2 mL
6 Tbsp.	sesame seed paste OR	100 mL
	unsalted smooth peanut butter	
3 Tbsp.	sugar	50 mL
1½ tsp.	salt	7 mL
2 Tbsp.	dark soy sauce	25 mL

1. Set a wok or skillet over high heat for 30 seconds. Add oil and heat for another 30 seconds. Add garlic, chilies and sesame seed paste and stir well.

2. Add sugar, salt and soy sauce and combine thoroughly.

3. Remove sauce from wok and allow to cool. Place in a 1-cup (250-mL) glass jar or ginger jar, label and refrigerate. Before presenting, attach Serving Suggestions and recipe for Cold Noodles with Sesame Seed Sauce.

Makes 1 cup (250 mL).

SERVING SUGGESTIONS
Follow recipe for Cold Noodles with Sesame Seed Sauce and serve as an hors d'oeuvre; or heat and serve with stir-fried chicken or meat as a dipping sauce. This sauce keeps two weeks in refrigerator or several months in freezer.

Cold Noodles with Sesame Seed Sauce

2 qts.	water	2 L
1 lb.	Chinese egg noodles	500 g
⅓ cup	Sesame Seed Sauce	75 mL
4 oz.	thinly sliced barbecued pork OR chicken	125 g
1 cup	fresh bean sprouts	250 mL

1. In a 4-quart (4-L) saucepan, bring water to boil over high heat. Drop in the noodles, bring back to the boil and cook for approximately 1 minute. Drain and rinse with cold water in a colander.

2. Place the cold noodles in a bowl and combine thoroughly with Sesame Seed Sauce. Arrange on a platter and sprinkle with barbecued pork and bean sprouts and serve cold.

Serves 4 to 6 as an hors d'oeuvre.

Black Bean Sauce

2 tsp.	vegetable OR peanut oil	10 mL
1	large garlic clove, finely chopped	1
15	dry fermented black beans	15
2 cups	water	500 mL
4 tsp.	sugar	20 mL
3 Tbsp.	dark soy sauce	50 mL
1¼ tsp.	salt	6 mL
4 tsp.	cornstarch, dissolved in	20 mL
¼ cup	cold water	50 mL

1. Set a wok or skillet over high heat for 30 seconds. Add oil, heat for a further 30 seconds and add garlic. Stir-fry for 30 seconds or until browned.

2. Add black beans and stir-fry for 20 seconds. Then stir in water, sugar, soy sauce and salt. Add cornstarch solution and bring to a boil, stirring until it thickens.

3. Remove sauce from wok, allow to cool, then label and refrigerate in 2 one-cup (250-mL) glass jars or ginger jars.

4. Before presenting, attach Serving Suggestions and recipe for Stir-Fried Prawns in Black Bean Sauce.

Makes 2 cups (500 mL).

SERVING SUGGESTIONS

Follow recipe for Stir-Fried Prawns in Black Bean Sauce or instead of prawns use chicken, beef, pork, lamb, seafood, vegetables or your favourite combination of the above. This sauce keeps 2 weeks in refrigerator or several months in freezer.

If the sauce is frozen, thaw, combine 4 tsp. (20 mL) cornstarch with ¼ cup (50 mL) cold water and pour into sauce and cook, stirring for 1 minute until sauce thickens.

Stir-Fried Prawns in Black Bean Sauce

2 Tbsp.	peanut OR vegetable oil	25 mL
1 lb.	fresh prawns, shelled and deveined OR frozen shrimp	500 g
½ cup	celery pieces, cut into ½-inch (1.5-cm) diagonal slices	125 mL
¼ cup	diced onions	50 mL
1	small carrot, cut into ¼-inch (6-mm) diagonal slices	1
½ cup	bite-sized pieces broccoli	125 mL
½ cup	Black Bean Sauce	125 mL

1. Set a wok or skillet over high heat for 30 seconds. Add oil and heat for 30 seconds. Add prawns and stir-fry for 1 minute.

2. Add vegetables and Black Bean Sauce, bring to a boil and stir-fry for 2 minutes. Transfer to a heated platter and serve at once.

Serves 2 as a main course. Serves 4 as one of several courses in a Chinese meal.

Szechuan Sauce

1 tsp.	peanut OR vegetable oil	5 mL
1	large garlic clove, finely chopped	1
1¾ cups	water	450 mL
1 Tbsp.	chili garlic sauce	15 mL
4 tsp.	Hoisin sauce	20 mL
1 Tbsp.	sugar	15 mL
1½ tsp.	salt	7 mL
2 Tbsp.	dark soy sauce	25 mL
4 tsp.	cornstarch dissolved in	20 mL
¼ cup	cold water	50 mL

1. Set a wok or skillet over high heat for 30 seconds. Add oil, heat for 30 seconds and add garlic. Stir-fry for 30 seconds or until browned. Add water and bring to a boil.

2. Add chili garlic sauce, Hoisin sauce, sugar, salt and soy sauce and return to the boil for 2 or 3 minutes. Add cornstarch solution and stir-fry for 1 minute or until it thickens. Bring to a boil and reduce for 2 minutes, stirring occasionally.

3. Remove the sauce from the wok and allow to cool. Place in 3 half-cup (125-mL) glass jars or ginger jars, label and refrigerate. Before presenting, attach Serving Suggestions and recipe for Stir-Fried Beef with Szechuan Sauce.

Makes 1½ cups (375 mL).

SERVING SUGGESTIONS

Follow recipe for Stir-Fried Beef with Szechuan Sauce, or substitute chicken, vegetables, pork, lamb, seafood or your favourite combination of the above. This sauce keeps 2 weeks in refrigerator or several months in freezer.

If the sauce is frozen, thaw, combine 4 tsp. (20 mL) cornstarch with ¼ cup (50 mL) cold water and pour into sauce and cook, stirring for 1 minute until sauce thickens.

Stir-Fried Beef with Szechuan Sauce

12 oz.	flank steak	350 g
1 tsp.	cornstarch	5 mL
2 tsp.	rice cooking wine	10 mL
¼ cup	water	50 mL
1 tsp.	sesame seed oil	5 mL
¼ tsp.	salt	1 mL
¼ tsp.	sugar	1 mL
2 Tbsp.	vegetable OR peanut oil	25 mL
½	medium sweet green pepper, seeded and cut into ½-inch (1.5-cm) pieces	½
6	water chestnuts, cut into ¼-inch (6-mm) pieces	6
1	medium carrot, scraped and cut into ¼-inch (6-mm) pieces	1
1 stalk	celery, cut into ¼-inch (6-mm) pieces	1 stalk
½ cup	Szechuan Sauce	125 mL

1. Place the steak in the freezer for approximately 30 minutes so that it will slice easily. Carve the steak against the grain into slices ⅛ inch (3 mm) thick.

2. Prepare a marinade by combining cornstarch, cooking wine, water, sesame seed oil, salt and sugar. Add steak and marinate 10 minutes.

3. Place a wok or skillet over high heat for 30 seconds. Add oil and heat a further 30 seconds. Add beef and marinade and stir-fry for 2 minutes.

4. Add vegetables and stir-fry for 1 minute.

5. Add Szechuan Sauce and bring to a boil. Transfer to a heated platter and serve immediately.

Serves 2 to 4 as a main course. Serves 4 to 6 as one of several courses in a Chinese meal.

TASTES OF SOUTHEAST ASIA

You can count on the cuisine of Southeast Asia for a touch of the exotic.

This dinner can be presented in a hibachi. Add bamboo skewers and a copy of *The Cuisines of Asia* by Jennifer Brennan. Your gift package might also contain rice vinegar (with the recipe for Thai Cucumber Salad), Nasi Goreng fried rice mix, krupek (a deep-fried shrimp chip available in bags or boxes), mangoes for dessert and green tea.

All the ingredients may be found in Chinatown or in stores specializing in Asian foods. These ingredients and substitutes are described below.

Bottled fish sauce is available in Chinese food shops.

Cilantro is also known as coriander or Chinese parsley.

Keffir lime leaves are used whole or ground to add a lemony flavour to many Southeast Asian curried dishes. Fresh lemon or lime leaves may be substituted.

Kha (laos root) is usually sold by the ounce in dried pieces; this root is related to ginger. If it is not available, you may substitute a mixture of 4 parts powdered ginger to 1 part powdered cinnamon or cardamom.

Lemongrass is a tall, grey-green grass with a scallionlike base and is one of the most important Thai flavourings. Powdered lemongrass is available in natural food stores and herb shops, where it is sold as a herb tea. If you use the powdered form, substitute 1 tsp. (5 mL) for each stalk of fresh grass. You may also use 1 tsp. (5 mL) finely grated lemon rind per stalk as a substitute.

Rice vinegar is a mild, sweet vinegar. If it is not available, substitute a mixture of 1 Tbsp. white vinegar and 1 Tbsp. water with 2 tsp. sugar (makes 2 Tbsp.).

Straw mushrooms come in cans. These mushrooms have pointed dark brown caps and short yellowish stems. They have a mild, delicate flavour and a slippery, silky texture.

Tamarind is a sour-tasting tropical fruit sold as dried pulp. To make tamarind water, mix 2 Tbsp. (25 mL) pulp with 1 cup (250 mL) boiling water and strain before use.

Thai chili paste. If you are unable to find this, you may use the chili paste available in Chinese markets. This fiery condiment is a staple in Szechuan cooking.

Before you start, read "About Chili Peppers" on p. 119.

Thai Cucumber Salad

1	long English cucumber	1
¼ cup	minced Bermuda onion	50 mL
2 Tbsp.	rice vinegar	25 mL
2 tsp.	minced fresh cilantro	10 mL
2 Tbsp.	chopped peanuts	25 mL

1. Slice the cucumber crosswise in thin rounds.
2. Place cucumbers in a serving bowl and toss with onion, vinegar and cilantro. Sprinkle the peanuts over the top.
3. This salad is best served within a few hours, but it can be refrigerated for serving within a day or two.

Makes 1 pint (500 mL). Serves 4–6.

Satay Sauce

5	dried whole red hot chilies	5
1	small onion, chopped	1
4 cloves	garlic, finely chopped	4 cloves
1¼ cups	water	300 mL
4 Tbsp.	peanut oil	60 mL
1½ cups	ground roasted peanuts	375 mL
2 Tbsp.	Demerara sugar	25 mL
1 Tbsp.	dark soy sauce	15 mL
1 tsp.	salt	5 mL
2 Tbsp.	tamarind water OR lemon juice	25 mL

1. Soak chilies in cold water to cover 1 hour or until softened. Remove chilies from water, seed and cut crosswise into small pieces.

2. Place chilies in food processor and add onion, garlic and ½ cup (125 mL) water. Blend thoroughly.

3. Place a wok or skillet over high heat for 30 seconds. Add oil and heat for another 30 seconds. Add chili mixture to wok and stir-fry for 3 minutes.

4. Add peanuts. Stir and add remaining water and bring to a boil. Add sugar, soy sauce, salt and tamarind water. Continue cooking for 20 minutes.

5. Pour into a wide-mouthed 3-cup (750-mL) canning jar, cool, label and refrigerate. Attach Serving Suggestion.

Makes 3 cups (750 mL).

SERVING SUGGESTION
Follow the attached recipe for Malaysian Lamb Satay.

Malaysian Lamb Satay

1 lb.	boneless lamb	500 g
2 tsp.	ground coriander	10 mL
½ tsp.	ground cumin	2 mL
½ tsp.	ground dried fennel	2 mL
½ tsp.	ground black pepper	2 mL
1 tsp.	turmeric	5 mL
3-inch length	fresh lemongrass,	7.5-cm length

trimmed and cut crosswise into
¼-inch (6-mm) pieces—about 2 Tbsp. (25 mL) OR

1 tsp.	lemongrass powder	5 mL
3 Tbsp.	coarsely chopped shallots	50 mL
1½ tsp.	finely minced garlic	7 mL
½ cup	water	125 mL
2 Tbsp.	sugar	25 mL
	salt to taste (optional)	
½ tsp.	Worcestershire sauce	2 mL
3 Tbsp.	peanut OR vegetable oil	45 mL
3 Tbsp.	canned coconut cream OR milk	45 mL

1. Put 30—36 wooden skewers in bowl and add cold water to cover. Soak 1 hour.

2. Preheat charcoal grill or broiler.

3. Cut lamb into ½-inch (1.3-cm) cubes; there should be about 2½ cups (625 mL). Put cubes in a bowl.

4. Sprinkle lamb with coriander, cumin, fennel, pepper and turmeric. Set aside.

5. Put lemongrass, shallots, garlic and water in a blender and blend thoroughly.

6. Pour blender mixture over the lamb and mix with the fingers. Add sugar, salt and Worcestershire sauce and blend. Set aside for 1 hour.

Throughout Southeast Asia, strips of chicken, lamb, beef and seafood are marinated, threaded on skewers and grilled. These kebabs are served as appetizers and also as a main course.

7. Add 1 Tbsp. (15 mL) of the oil to the lamb mixture and blend well.

8. Drain skewers and thread 4—6 pieces of lamb on each skewer, arranging them close together.

9. Blend remaining 2 Tbsp. (30 mL) oil with coconut cream.

10. Arrange skewered lamb on charcoal grill or under broiler. Cook 4—6 minutes, depending on whether it is to be medium-cooked or well done. Turn skewers to cook evenly. As meat cooks, brush generously with oil and coconut mixture.

11. Serve with warm Satay Sauce for dipping.
Serves 6.

Southern-style Picnic Basket: In the basket are Hot Pepper Jelly, peanuts, and Cajun Drumsticks packed in popcorn; in front are Cornbread Buttermilk Muffins, Bell Pepper Butter, Peanut Pie and Jalapeño Potato Salad; to the right are canning jars of Cajun Martinis and iced tea. Add a copy of *Gone with the Wind,* a bunch of spring wildflowers and wear a straw hat.

Lemon Shrimp Soup

1 Tbsp.	Thai chili paste	15 mL
2½ cups	chicken broth	625 mL
1 stalk	fresh lemongrass,	1 stalk
	cut into 1-inch (2.5-cm) sections	
2	keffir lime leaves	2
2 slices	kha (laos root)	2 slices
1 Tbsp.	bottled fish sauce, to taste	15 mL
2 Tbsp.	lime juice	25 mL
12	fresh shrimp OR prawns, shelled	12
6	fresh whole red chilies	6
8	canned straw mushrooms, cut in half	8
1 stalk	fresh cilantro, leaves only	1 stalk
1	small onion, cut into small pieces	1

Lemon Shrimp Soup is the Thai national soup and this excellent version is from the Bangkok Garden Restaurant in Toronto.

1. Combine chili paste and broth in a saucepan and bring to a boil. Add lemongrass, lime leaves, kha, fish sauce and lime juice and return to boil.

2. Add shrimp and continue to cook for 1 minute. Remove from heat immediately so that shrimp do not overcook.

3. Taste for seasonings: to increase the saltiness, add more fish sauce; to increase the sourness, add more lime juice. Crush or gently pound the fresh chilies.

4. Add chilies, mushrooms, cilantro and onion.

5. Pour soup into 1 four-cup (1-L) thermos bottle that has been heated with boiling water; or cool and refrigerate until ready to present gift, then pour into thermos and heat just before serving.

Serves 4.

West Coast Dinner features West Coast Shellfish Pizzas, California Pot au Feu and Citrus Fruit Bread Pudding. The small pot contains Pesto. Include a California or British Columbia wine, wine glasses and a pizza cutter. The market basket contains a West Coast lifestyle magazine.

SOUTHERN-STYLE PICNIC BASKET

Recreate generous southern hospitality with a bright yellow picnic basket packed with homemade specialties. Add a bunch of mint, some colourful bandanas for napkins and perhaps two plastic martini glasses.

Your food package might contain the Cajun Martini bottle, Cajun Spice Mix with a recipe for Cajun Drumsticks, Hot Pepper Jelly (p. 36), Bell Pepper Butter (p. 69), Jalapeño Potato Salad, Cornbread Buttermilk Muffins, Peanut Pie and a thermos of iced tea.

Before you start, read "About Chili Peppers" on p. 119.

Cajun Martini

4	fresh jalapeño peppers	4
26-oz. bottle	vodka	750-mL bottle

1. Add peppers to vodka bottle and steep 4 days. Remove peppers and store vodka in freezer.
2. Add to picnic basket with an ice pack and serve cold.

Jalapeño Potato Salad

3 lbs.	new potatoes, scrubbed but not peeled	1.5 kg
4	hard-boiled eggs, thinly sliced	4
1 stalk	celery, diced	1 stalk
½ cup	thinly sliced green onions	125 mL
¼ cup	diced sweet green pepper	50 mL
¼ cup	diced sweet red pepper	50 mL
2	fresh OR canned jalapeño peppers, finely chopped	2
	salt and pepper	
½ cup	mayonnaise	125 mL
½ cup	sour cream	125 mL
1 Tbsp.	Dijon mustard	15 mL

1. Boil potatoes in salted water to cover for 20 minutes or until tender when pierced with a fork. Drain, cool slightly and cut into ½-inch (1.5-cm) slices.

2. Combine potatoes, eggs, celery, green onions and peppers in a large bowl. Add salt and pepper and gently toss.

3. In a separate bowl combine mayonnaise, sour cream and mustard and gently fold into potato mixture. Taste and correct seasonings. Store in a 1-quart (1-L) canning jar, label and refrigerate.

Serves 6–8.

Cajun Spice Mix

3 Tbsp.	cayenne pepper	50 mL
1 Tbsp.	white pepper	15 mL
1 Tbsp.	black pepper	15 mL
2 Tbsp.	cocoa powder	25 mL
2 Tbsp.	ground cumin	25 mL
2 Tbsp.	dry mustard	25 mL
2 Tbsp.	onion powder	25 mL
2 Tbsp.	garlic powder	25 mL
2 Tbsp.	paprika	25 mL
3 Tbsp.	salt	50 mL
1 Tbsp.	ground cinnamon	15 mL
1 Tbsp.	thyme	15 mL
1 Tbsp.	oregano	15 mL
1 Tbsp.	basil	15 mL

Combine all ingredients, store in a 1-cup (250-mL) airtight container and label.

Makes 1 cup (250 mL).

SERVING SUGGESTIONS
Follow directions for Cajun Drumsticks, or rub mix into beef or fish before sautéing. For best flavour use within 6 months.

Cajun Drumsticks

12	chicken drumsticks	12
¼ cup	all-purpose flour	50 mL
1 cup	Cajun Spice Mix	250 mL
¾ cup	peanut oil	175 mL

1. Preheat oven to 375°F (190°C).
2. Rinse and pat dry chicken.
3. Mix flour with 1 Tbsp. (15 mL) spice mix in paper or plastic bag.
4. Rub remaining spice mix evenly over chicken, rubbing in well.
5. Heat oil in a large skillet to 365°F (185°C).
6. Shake chicken in flour and spice mixture until well coated.
7. Cook chicken in oil, uncovered, 8 minutes on each side or until golden. Drain on paper towels.
8. Place in shallow baking dish and bake for 30 minutes.
Serves 6.

Cornbread Buttermilk Muffins

¾ cup	cornmeal	175 mL
1¼ cups	unbleached flour	300 mL
4 oz.	extra-old cheddar cheese, grated	125 g
1 Tbsp.	baking powder	15 mL
½ tsp.	salt	2 mL
1 tsp.	crushed red pepper flakes (optional)	5 mL
2	eggs	2
½ cup	oil	125 mL
¾ cup	buttermilk	175 mL

1. Preheat oven to 375°F (190°C) and butter muffin pan.
2. Combine cornmeal, flour, cheese, baking powder, salt and red pepper flakes in a medium-sized mixing bowl.
3. In a separate bowl, beat eggs and stir in oil and buttermilk. Add liquid to dry ingredients and combine just until moistened.
4. Fill greased muffin pan and bake for 15 minutes or until golden brown.
5. Wrap muffins in foil or individually in plastic wrap. Include Serving Suggestion.

Makes 12 muffins.

SERVING SUGGESTION
Serve with Bell Pepper Butter.

Peanut Pie

PECAN CRUST

2 cups	ground pecans	500 mL
2 Tbsp.	brown sugar	25 mL
1	extra-large egg white, beaten until frothy	1
2 tsp.	powdered ginger	10 mL
	zest of ½ orange	

Combine all ingredients and press into bottom of 9- or 10-inch (1-L) pie plate and chill.

PEANUT FILLING

8 oz.	cream cheese	250 g
¾ cup	smooth peanut butter	175 mL
1 cup	icing sugar	250 mL
½ cup	light cream	125 mL
1 tsp.	vanilla	5 mL
1 cup	whipping cream, whipped	250 mL
¾ cup	unsalted, blanched peanuts	175 mL

1. Place cream cheese, peanut butter, sugar, light cream and vanilla into a food processor with a metal blade and blend thoroughly.

2. Place batter in a bowl and fold in whipped cream.

3. Add peanuts, pour into prepared crust and refrigerate or freeze.

WEST COAST DINNER

Created by Executive Chef Kerry Sear of the Four Seasons Hotel in Vancouver, this menu reflects the best of the West Coast. Fresh seafood—clams, mussels, crabmeat and prawns—is a topping for small pizzas. California Pot au Feu combines chicken, duck and veal with baby vegetables. Serve with orzo (a pasta shaped like grains of rice) tossed with butter and Parmesan cheese to taste. For dessert, West Coast cooks like to prepare comfort foods, and nothing is more comforting than Sear's innovative Citrus Fruit Bread Pudding (p. 76) with Crème Fraîche (p. 75), the perfect ending to a West Coast soirée.

To make up your gift package, follow the recipe for Herb Pizza Dough and prebake the pizza shells, stack them between gold doilies and tie up with a bright ribbon; add a glass measuring cup or jar filled with homemade Pesto and attach the recipe for West Coast Shellfish Pizza. (You may wish to purchase pizza dough mix and pesto rather than make them yourself.) You can, if you wish, make the Pot au Feu ahead and freeze it. Put in a package of orzo with serving instructions. Present the pudding ready to bake in a white porcelain soufflé or pudding mould, and the Crème Fraîche in a jar. You may want to add a clay baker as part of the gift.

Fill a pastel market basket or a twig basket with this dinner, adding a bottle of California or British Columbia wine and épi baguettes. Include a book of Haida legends, a Bryan Adams tape, a West Coast lifestyle magazine or *Gifts from the Kitchen*.

West Coast Shellfish Pizza

HERB PIZZA DOUGH

3 cups	unbleached flour	750 mL
1 tsp.	fresh basil	5 mL
1 tsp.	fresh oregano	5 mL
1 Tbsp.	dry yeast	15 mL
½ cup	warm water	125 mL
	at 105–115°F (41–46°C)	
1 cup	warm milk	250 mL
2 Tbsp.	olive oil	25 mL
1½ tsp.	salt	7 mL
	cornmeal	
	freshly ground black pepper	

1. Measure flour, basil and oregano into a large mixing bowl or food processor and blend.

2. Sprinkle yeast into warm water and let stand until foamy and dissolved, about 10 minutes.

3. *If mixing by hand,* make a well in the centre of the flour, pour in the dissolved yeast mixture, add the warm milk and stir with a wooden spoon. Add the olive oil and salt, mixing until all the flour and liquids are combined, then turn dough out onto a lightly floured surface and knead gently until it is smooth and satiny, about 10 minutes.

If using a food processor, turn machine on and pour yeast mixture and warm milk through the feed tube. Process until a ball of dough forms, then add the oil and salt and process 40 seconds until it is smooth. Turn dough out onto a lightly floured surface.

4. Cover dough with a mixing bowl and let rise. It should double in volume in 2½–3 hours.

To simulate a pizza oven, line your oven rack with unglazed quarry tiles or a baking stone. Always preheat your oven at least 30 minutes.

5. Punch the dough down and knead several times. Divide it into 8 pieces, form the pieces into balls and flour lightly. Cover with a towel and let the balls rise (about 10 minutes). At this point, dough may be refrigerated for 3 days or may be frozen. Bring to room temperature before proceeding.

6. Preheat oven to 450°F (230°C). Lightly sprinkle a heavy pizza pan or baking pan with cornmeal. Flatten each dough ball into a flat disc and then roll or stretch the dough until 6 inches (15 cm) in diameter, making the edges thicker.

7. Brush lightly with olive oil to help keep crisp. Grind fresh pepper onto each pizza. Bake for 7 minutes.

PESTO

2 cups	firmly packed fresh basil leaves	500 mL
½ cup	fresh parsley	125 mL
½ cup	walnuts OR pine nuts	125 mL
3 cloves	garlic	3 cloves
¾ cup	extra-virgin olive oil	200 mL
1 cup	Parmesan cheese OR	250 mL
½ cup	each Parmesan and Romano cheese	125 mL
1 tsp.	salt	1 mL
	freshly ground pepper	

1. Combine basil, parsley, nuts and garlic in a blender or food processor. With the motor running, add oil in a steady stream, scraping down sides of container with a spatula.

2. Add cheese, salt and pepper and mix.

3. Keeps refrigerated for 1 week or freeze.

Makes 2 cups (500 mL).

SHELLFISH TOPPING

½ cup	raspberry vinegar	125 mL
2 Tbsp.	sugar	25 mL
1 clove	garlic, crushed	1 clove
3	large red onions, thinly sliced	3
4	large tomatoes, peeled, seeded and diced	4

16	little-neck clams, in shells	16
16	mussels, in shells	16
8 Tbsp.	Pesto	120 mL
16	fresh prawns, tail cleaned, head left on	16
8	large scallops	8
½ lb.	fresh crabmeat, divided into 8 portions	250 g
	freshly ground pepper	
16	fresh oregano stems	16
	fresh nasturtium leaves, cut into thin strips (optional)	
½ cup	sour cream	125 mL
2 oz.	smoked salmon, chopped	60 g
	chives	
	olive oil	

1. In a heavy saucepan over medium heat, combine vinegar, sugar and garlic. Reduce by half. Add onions and cover. Cook until tender and liquid has evaporated. Fold in tomatoes and allow to cool.

2. Blanch clams and mussels in boiling water until they open (about 30 seconds) and rinse immediately with cold water. Set aside.

3. Spread 1 Tbsp. (15 mL) Pesto on each pizza. Place a small amount of onion-tomato mixture in the centre of each pizza and arrange clams, mussels, prawns, scallops and crabmeat around it.

4. Season with pepper and arrange oregano and nasturtium on top. Bake for 5−7 minutes or until the edges are puffy and light brown.

5. Meanwhile, mix sour cream, smoked salmon and chives in a small bowl.

6. When pizza is cooked, brush seafood with olive oil and garnish with a spoonful of sour cream mixture. Serve immediately.

Makes 8 appetizer pizzas.

California Pot au Feu

Have your butcher debone the ducks, remove excess fat and cut them into the same size as the chicken pieces.

½ bunch	fresh cilantro, finely chopped	½ bunch
1 bunch	fresh thyme, finely chopped	1 bunch
4	chicken thighs, skinned, deboned and cut in half	4
1 lb.	boneless veal shoulder, cut into 2-inch (5-cm) chunks	500 g
2	prepared ducks, 3–4 lbs. (1.5–2 kg) each	2
3 Tbsp.	vegetable oil	50 mL
¼ lb.	butter	125 g
1	red onion, sliced	1
1 clove	garlic, crushed	1 clove
8	whole green onions	8
½	medium red pepper, diced	½
½	medium yellow pepper, diced	½
2 qt.	chicken stock	2 L
8	baby zucchini OR	8
1	medium zucchini, cut diagonally into ½-inch (1.5-cm) slices	1
8	baby yellow crookneck squash OR	8
1	medium yellow crookneck squash, cut diagonally into ½-inch (1.5-cm) slices	1
8	baby pattypan squash OR	8
1	medium pattypan squash, cut diagonally into ½-inch (1.5-cm) slices	1
8	baby corn-on-the-cob	8
	freshly ground black pepper	
¼ cup	fresh garlic chives, chopped	50 mL
½ bunch	fresh cilantro, chopped	½ bunch
½ lb.	fresh shiitake mushrooms, sliced	250 g

1. Combine cilantro and thyme in a small bowl. In a glass container, pat herbs on chicken, veal and duck and cover with plastic wrap. Refrigerate overnight.

2. Preheat oven to 350°F (180°C). In a heavy skillet over high heat, heat oil and sear chicken, veal and duck to brown all sides. Remove from pan and set aside.

3. Rinse skillet and place over medium heat. Put in half the butter to melt. Add red onion, garlic and whole green onions and sauté until onions are translucent but not browned. Add the peppers and the chicken stock, bring to a boil and simmer until liquid is reduced by half.

4. In a large casserole, alternate layers of chicken, veal and duck with vegetables, seasoning each with black pepper, chopped garlic chives and cilantro. Pour the onion-stock mixture over all, then add the shiitake mushrooms and remaining butter.

5. Cover and cook for one hour, skimming foam and fat.

Serves 8.

KITCHEN TECHNIQUES

About Metric Measure

All recipes in this book give both imperial and metric measurements. For best results use one or the other, but do not use both and do not convert recipes yourself. Because recipes do not follow conversion tables strictly, indicated measures often are not consistent or precisely equivalent.

About Flours

Stone-ground wholewheat flour and unbleached flour are available in health food stores, supermarkets and specialty shops. Be sure to use the type of flour specified in each recipe.

Some of these recipes call for self-raising flour. If you do not have this, you may prepare it by combining:

1 cup	all-purpose flour	250 mL
1½ tsp.	baking powder	7 mL
½ tsp.	salt	2 mL

About Chili Peppers

A word of warning: Cooking chili peppers tends to intensify their heat. The seeds and the veins are the hottest parts of a chili. Chilies exude a volatile oil, so you should wear rubber gloves when handling them. Always wash your hands after handling hot peppers and be careful not to touch your eyes.

About Canning

Canning means preserving foods in glass jars. Use jars that are specially designed for home canning. Coffee and salad-dressing jars are not strong enough to withstand the heat of processing, nor are their lids always airtight. Use glass canning jars with two-piece vacuum caps (a metal lid edged with sealing compound and a metal screw band). Always use new metal lids (or new rubber rings if you use glass-lidded jars), since the canning process warps them.

Use a water bath canner or a kettle with a tight-fitting lid and a wire, metal or wooden rack that lets water circulate under the jars. The canner must be deep enough so that the water will cover the jars.

Follow the steps below.

PREPARING THE JARS

1. Examine jars, lids, rubber rings and screw bands carefully. Discard any that are damaged.
2. Wash them in hot soapy water and rinse with boiling water, or put them through a dishwasher cycle.
3. Prepare metal lids according to manufacturer's directions. Do not boil longer than specified.
4. Invert rinsed jars in a bath canner or kettle in simmering water to cover, and keep the equipment in the water until you are ready to fill the jars.

FILLING THE JARS

5. When you are ready to fill the jars, remove them from the water.
6. As you fill the jars, leave the headspace recommended in each recipe.
7. Remove all air bubbles by running a knife blade around the inside and down the centre of each jar.

8. Carefully wipe the top edge of each jar with a damp cloth before sealing and screw the band on only until finger-tip tight. Overtightening prevents lids from sealing properly.

PROCESSING THE FOOD

Always process food immediately after closing the jars, while the food and jars are still hot.

9. Make sure that the canner is only half-full of water at about the same temperature as that of the jars.

10. Put in the jars about 2 inches (5 cm) apart.

11. Add hot water until it rises at least 2 inches (5 cm) above the tops of the jars.

12. Cover the canner tightly and bring the water to a boil. Time the processing from the moment the water reaches a rolling boil. Keep the water boiling vigorously and add more boiling water if necessary to maintain the proper depth. Process for exact times given in the recipe.

COOLING, TESTING AND STORING CANNED FOOD

13. When processing is complete, use tongs to remove the jars immediately to avoid overcooking. Place the jars upright on a wire rack, or on folded dry cloth or newspapers.

14. When the jars have cooled, test the metal lids by tapping them gently with a spoon; if well sealed, there is a clear, ringing sound and lids curve slightly inward.

15. Wipe the jars with a damp cloth, dry them thoroughly and label them with name, date and note to refrigerate after opening. Store them in a cool, dark, dry place. Wait at least 10 days before using canned foods so that flavours may ripen.

About Tempering Chocolate

For best results, chocolate should be tempered. Tempering is the process of heating chocolate to a temperature between 110°F and 120°F (43°C and 49°C), a range high enough to melt the cocoa butter crystals completely. This ensures that the chocolate will have a high gloss, a smooth texture, a crisp snap when broken, and an even colour, without a whitish film. Tempering may be done in a double boiler or in a microwave oven. Both methods require 1¼ lbs. (625 g) of chocolate, ¼ lb. (125 g) in a solid chunk and the rest coarsely chopped and divided into two ½-lb. (250-g) batches.

DOUBLE BOILER METHOD

1. Fill the bottom half of a double boiler with enough water to touch the bottom and sides of the top half. Heat the water to a temperature of 125°F (52°C) and maintain this temperature during melting. Insert the top half containing ½ lb. (250 g) of chopped chocolate.

2. Let the chocolate stand a few minutes until it begins to melt, then stir it and gradually add the remaining ½ lb. (250 g) of chopped chocolate. Dark chocolate should be stirred frequently, milk chocolate almost constantly, and white chocolate continuously to ensure complete and even melting.

3. Heat the melted chocolate until it reaches 110–120°F (43–49°C) on a chocolate thermometer. Pour the chocolate into a 1-quart (1-L) bowl.

4. Add the ¼ lb. (125 g) of solid chocolate and stir slowly and continuously until the temperature drops to the optimum dipping temperature (see below).

5. Remove the solid piece of chocolate. Place the bowl on an electric heating pad wrapped in a thin tea towel and set at low. The chocolate is ready for dipping.